आनन्दाद्ध्येव खल्विमानि भूतानि जायन्ते,
आनन्देन जातानि जीवन्ति ।
आनन्दं प्रयन्त्यभिसंविशन्ति ।

"From Pure Joy springs all creation;
by Joy it is sustained, towards joy it
proceeds and to Joy it returns."

Plates 1 and 2

Devi Ambika. From an illuminated Ms. Rajasthan. c. 17th century A.D.
Devi as Mula Prakriti, Primal Energy, is *abyakta*, the indistinguishable
one, the whole cosmic process dissolved and returned to its pure
existence. According to Yoginihridaya Tantra: "Obeisance be to Her
who is Pure Being—Consciousness—Bliss, as Power, who exists
in the form of Time and Space and all that is therein, and who is the
radiant illuminatrix in all beings." By unfolding, that pure consciousness, that principle which stays forever motionless, yet acts
through its own radiations, the creative impulse is again activated.

॥श्रीअंबिकादेवता

Ajit Mookerjee

TANTRA ASANA

a way to self-realization

Published by Ravi Kumar   *Basel · Paris · New Delhi*

By the same author:
Folk Art of Bengal, Museum Studies,
The Arts of India, Folk Toys of India,
Modern Art in India, Indian Primitive Art,
Tantra Art, Tantra Kunst (German Ed.)

Library of Congress Catalogue Card Number 79-15 3698
Literary and reproduction rights reserved for all countries
© Copyright 1971 by Ravi Kumar,
Basilius Presse, CH 4002 Basel, Switzerland
34, Avenue Président Kennedy, Paris 16e
Kumar Gallery, Sundarnagar, New Delhi

I am still in search, after 22 years. I have looked for it in this land of saktis stretching from the Himalayas to the seas. Once the sadhakas, in their striving to do the world good, attained knowledge of even the source of creation through their dedication to the supreme, the one and indivisible Sakti. Where are those sadhakas now? Where can one hear this incantation:

त्वं स्वाहा त्वं स्वधा त्वं हि वषट्कारः स्वरात्मिका ।

I set out to rediscover those sacred spots where yogins meditated and succeeded in attaining to siddhi and there is no road back for me. Somewhere in this great land sacrificial fires are still being fed to attain the knowledge which seeks to grasp the still centre of the everchanging universe. Some sadhakas somewhere must be going all out to know the mysterious supreme power who is at the root of the creation, balance and dissolution. Where is that person who, hidden somewhere, has looked for her and been able to pronounce that Sakti is Consciousness!
I salute that Consciousness.
The subject matter of tantric asana is very difficult and is rather misconceived because of its apparently paradoxical nature—earthly and transcendental. To put the subject into present form, I am indebted to Samar Sen, Ravi Kumar, Dr. Kalyan Ganguly for their cooperation.

A. M.

To Me and Thee

Plate 3 →

AING, AING is Thy favourite mantra,
Thou who art both form and formlessness,
Who art the wealth of the lotus face
of the lotus-born,
Embodiment of all gunas, yet devoid of
attributes,
Changeless, and neither gross nor subtle.

None know Thy nature, nor is Thy inner
reality known.
Thou art the whole universe;
And Thou it is who existeth within it.
Thou art saluted by the foremost of Devas.
Without part Thou existeth in Thy fulness
everywhere.
Ever pure art Thou.

Sarasvatistotra (Tantrasara)

← Plate 3
Vak-devi. Painting. Rajasthan. c. 17th century A.D.
Nada or Sound that never ends, symbolizing the goddess Sarasvati,
stands for *vak* or the subtle element of sound. Nada is regarded as
eternal, absolute and self-contained. This Sound is Sphota in the
Tantric code; it is the creative principle of the universe. The goddess
is all white and her body is adorned with sages, celestial beings,
gods and goddesses. Upon her forehead rests Brahma, the creator
and Vishnu, the preserver, on her navel.

"The woman you love, you must not possess"

Goddess Basholi

To attain the state of perfect bliss is the ultimate aim of Tantra. Our ordinary pleasure experiences are of an extremely limited nature—they afford but fleeting glimpses of supreme joy—and this ephemeral quality will always send us back to a gross plane, preventing the advance towards self-realization.

Tantra asana is one of the means of this realization. The asanas, the science of psycho-yogic poses, are based upon the conception of the universe and of man's role in it. To become aware of one's own incredible potential, to realize and experience joy in being one with the cosmos—this is the fulfilment of asana.

It is a yogic practice of transcending the human condition. Tantra itself is unique for being a synthesis of bhoga and yoga, enjoyment and liberation. There is no place for renunciation or denial in Tantra. Instead, we must involve ourselves in all the life processes which surround us. The spiritual is not something that descends from above, rather it is an illumination that is to be discovered within.

Also fundamental in Tantrism is the notion of identity of the human body (anda, the power that binds the matter), the microcosm, with the universe or macrocosm (brahmanda). Tantra holds that the body is the abode of truth, the epitome of the universe; and so man contains within himself, the truth of the whole cosmos. Therefore, the body, with its physiological and physical processes, becomes the perfect medium (yantra) to attain truth. "He who realizes the truth of the body can then come to know the truth of the universe", says Ratnasara.

The creative process according to Tantrism.

Tantra asana is a method used to unite the individual self (Atman) with the Absolute Infinite (Brahman) in the cosmic-conscious state known as samadhi. Here there is only Pure Existence, Siva-Sakti, where the formed and formless are unified and merged. It is the state of Sat-Chit-Ananda, that is, Pure Existence-Consciousness-Bliss.

Before creation there was unity. Creation disrupted this unity and gave rise to multiplicity. Only through a return to the primal unity can one know the freedom of the Absolute. And to attain this freedom, we must integrate the principle of male-female. Whether achieved within one's body, or through the union of two bodies, the goal is always the reunification of the two principles. Man and woman are the mould of ultimate expression: the one which becomes two constantly aspires to become one again.

In the beginning there is the One—that infinite existence which transcends all states. In Pure Existence is Sakti, omnipotent, and Sabda (inaudible form of cosmic sound), omnipresent. From Sound as the basis of creation, Bindu (point-limit) appeared. In this infinitely vast inner space, all times—past, present and future—are contracted into Bindu: two Bindus as the state of creation (srishti), three Bindus as the state of continuance (sthiti) and the return to one Bindu as the state of absorption (laya) are condensed in a dot. It is the immovable centre around which the manifest world gravitates.

The centre is Adya-Sakti, Kali, the Black-One, with her three gunas (qualities), Sattva (essence), Rajas (activity), and Tamas (inertia) remaining in equilibrium. She is the Mother of Time for in Time (Kala) everything exists, is sustained and dissolves. Hence time to Tantrics is not continuous, but is repeatedly coming to an end to begin its cycle once again. Kali is dense darkness, the most intensely concentrated (ghanibhuta) light, one that is not vibrant, a background against which phenomenal light-forms become visible. She is the Mother-principle which governs the unfolding of the life process. When Sakti opens herself, the universe comes to be and when she closes, the universe dissolves. For, 'I am, out of me all things originate' and 'into me all are withdrawn.' Thus the cosmic Mother-principle is manifest even on our scale of being. Just as the human foetus is surrounded by a life-giving fluid, so it is with Brahmanda. The Cosmic Egg is placed in an infinite ocean of energy or Universal Rita from which the life-principle is sustained.

In the equilibrium of Sakti's three gunas, a throbbing tension arose, a spontaneous vibration so great that it agitated Sattva, Rajas and Tamas. Sattva is the illuminating force which releases consciousness, Rajas is the activity of attraction or repulsion, and Tamas is inactivity, the heaviest of the gunas, a state of condensation of energy in matter.

Rajas breaks the harmony as the trilogy becomes energized for the sake of creation. Dynamic forces are released stirring all latent existence in Brahmanda, the embryonic state of the universe.

The nature of this agitation is the process of contraction and expansion in which the encircling space and non-space, lokaloka, are manifest. These are the basis of creation, from the invisible atom to the vastness of the universe from the microscopic cell to the fully developed organism.

A study in Tantric physiology.

In the human body, there are several energy centres containing latent psychic powers. These are called chakras. If activated, they hold potential for reaching cosmic planes of awareness. They can be portals into a new existence and the realization of inherent powers.

The six main chakras of the human body are the Muladhara Chakra (at the base of the spine), Svadhisthana (near the generative organ), Manipura (near the navel), Anahata (near the heart), Visuddha (near the throat) and Ajna (between the brows). A seventh chakra, situated four fingers above the cerebrum, is Sahasrara, symbolically represented by the thousand-petalled lotus. Sahasrara is said to be the abode of Siva, cosmic consciousness, and Muladhara the seat of Sakti, whose form is that of a cosmic force known as Kundalini. Ultimately, Tantra asana aims to arouse the Kundalini Sakti to unite with Siva, realizing the highest, most intense joy—mahasukha.

The human body also contains five sheaths or koshas. According to Tantra, only one third of the human body is in evidence—the rest is invisible. The five sheaths are: (1) Anna-maya, (2) Prana-maya, (3) Manomaya, (4) Vijnana-maya, (5) Ananda-maya. The physical sheath of the body is called the Anna-maya kosha, with earth, water and fire elements having their functions in the Muladhara, Svadhisthana and Manipura chakras.

Prana-maya is the sheath of the vital air. It holds the life-force. Prana, which expresses itself in the form of air and space. These elements control the Anahata and Visuddha psychic centres.

Mano-maya and Vijnana-maya koshas are identified with the cognitive principle; the Ajna chakra is their centre. When it is revealed, one gets the inner vision, a simultaneous knowledge of things as they really are and the third eye opens in the centre of the forehead.

All the six centres (sat-chakras) are located within the Meru-danda (the vertebral column), not in the gross (sthula-sharira) but in the subtle body (linga-sharira). As repositories of psychic energies, they govern the whole condition of being. However, in man's normal state, these chakras are dormant.

Through planned meditative asanas, Kundalini Sakti, the great power within the human body, usually latent, is awakened. This force is compared to a snake lying asleep in the subtle body. Once released from the Muladhara Chakra, she uncoils herself and begins to rise upward, breaking open and transforming each energy centre as she ascends until Sakti enters the magnetic sphere of Siva-consciousness.

In yogic practice, discipline of breathing is absolutely essential. Prana, the life-force, or vital air, enters the human entity through these psychic centres and nadis (channels in the subtle body), diffusing throughout according to different functions. These are known as vayus (vital airs) which are important to the Tantric practitioner.

सत्त्व

"That aspect (Rupa) of Devi which is the Supreme Bliss and the Great Cause of the worlds neither appears nor disappears"

Gandharva-Tantra

Plate 4
OM. Painting. Kangra, Himachal Pradesh. c. 18th century A.D.
The cosmic sound, OM is the combination of the three matras,
a, *u* and *m*, which stand for the beginning of creation.

Plate 5
Anantanag. Painting. Kangra, Himachal Pradesh. c. 18th century A.D.
The serpent power symbolizes the source of all cosmic energy that
can create, sustain, and destroy the entire structure of the universe
through the immeasurable range and intensity of its power.

Plate 6
Cosmic Sun. Painting, Kangra, Himachal Pradesh. c. 18th century A.D.
The cosmic sun gives birth to the phenomenal world which embodies
the reflected images of forms created and produced by the radiant light.

Plate 7
Ekarnava Flood. Painting. Kangra, Himachal Pradesh.
c. 18th century A.D.
The Ekarnava Glacial Flood is said to occur at the end of the sixth
Manvantara period. The symbolism of boat floating in the Ekarnava
ocean means the seeds protected for the sake of creation and the fish
represents the emergence of life from the waters.

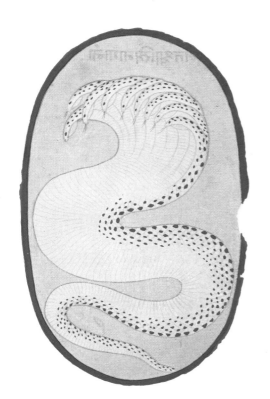

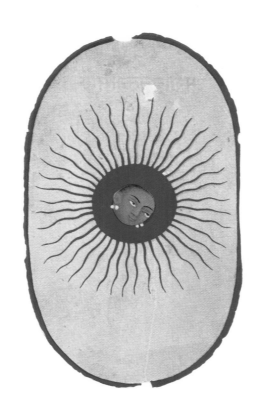

Plate 8
Expanding Universe. Drawing. Rajasthan. c. 18th century A.D.
The Bindu is a point out of time and space, the "area" in which
samadhi is experienced. The universe conceived either as the most
minute or as the encompassing Brahma-spheroid consists of a *sveta*
or white bindu and a *rakta* or red bindu intimately connected. It is the
fundamental point of repose out of which emerge transformation
and evolution. It signifies the starting point in the unfolding of inner
space, as well as the last point of its ultimate integration. It is the
point-limit from which inner and outer space take their origin and
in which they again become one.

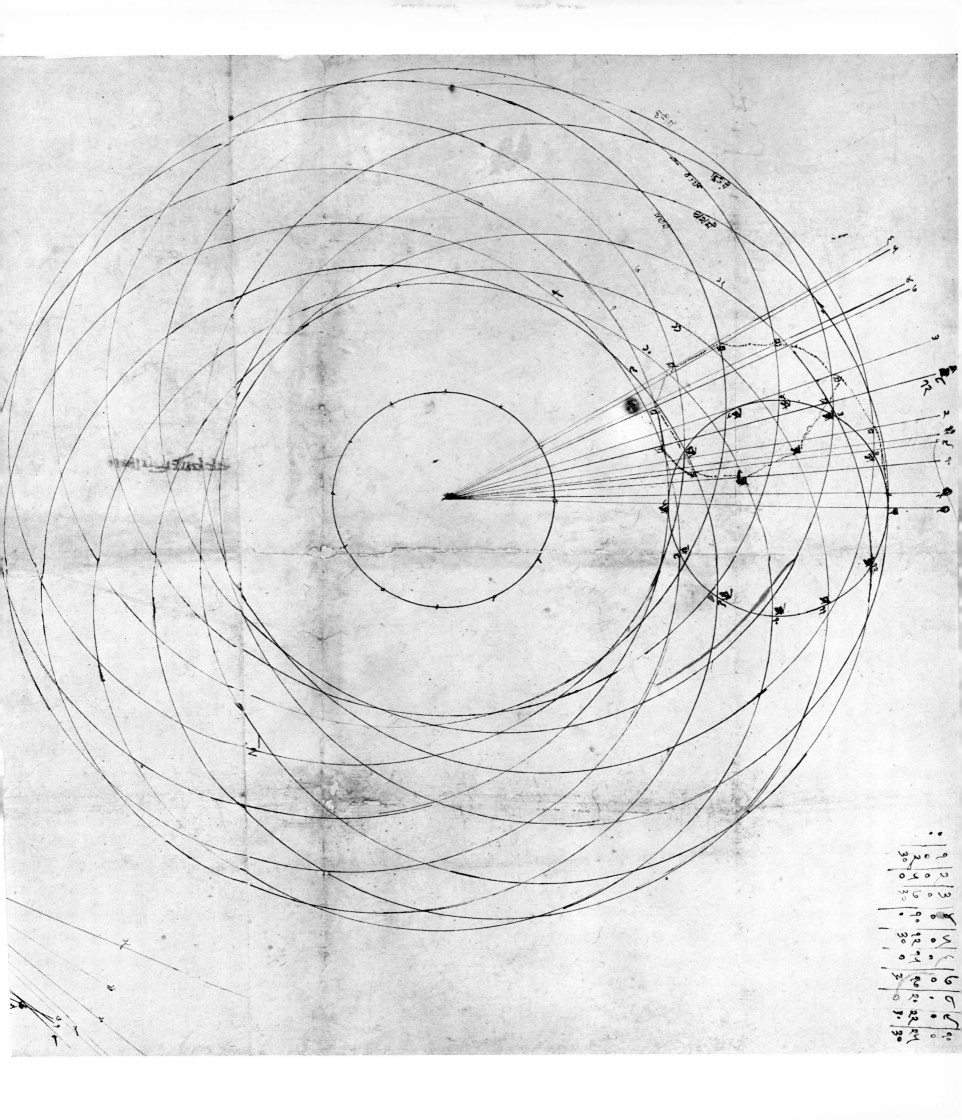

Plate 9
Brahmanda. Stone. c. 17th century A.D.
According to the Tantras, the different spheres of Brahmanda extend
through the cosmos to reach the transcosmic plane merging into
the ultimate stillness, *aloka*, the non-universe which is free from all
gunas (qualities).

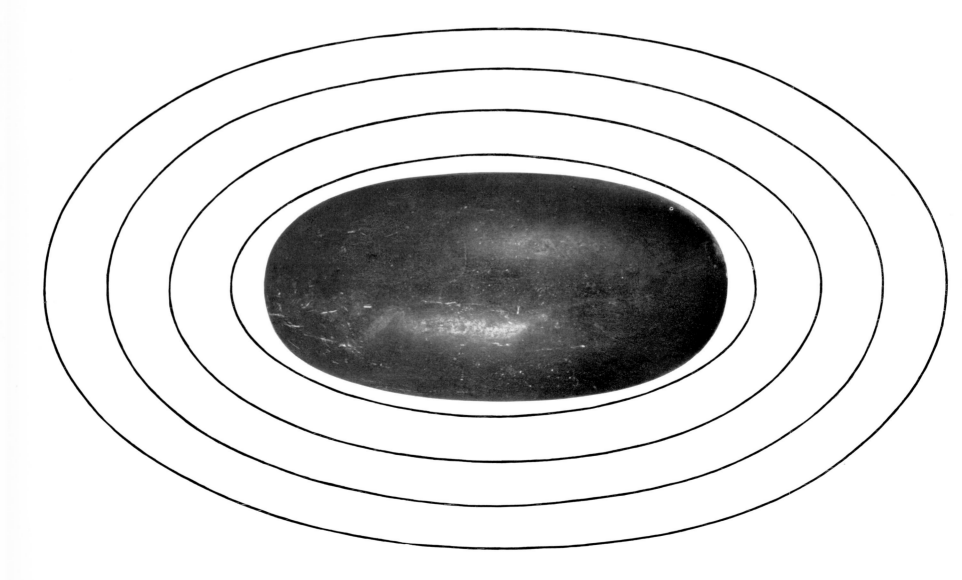

Plate 10
Cosmogram. From an illuminated Ms. Gujarat. c. 16th century A.D.
The concept of the universe comprises both its creation as well as
its dissolution. Brahmanda, the cosmic egg, contains the twenty-one
lokas conceived in three successive strata known as the *triloka* or three
worlds.

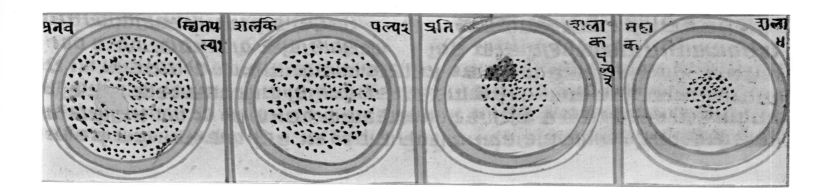

Plate 11
Lokas. Painting. Rajasthan. c. 17th century A.D.
From a Sangrahanisutra Ms.
The lunar and the solar regions include the atmospheric spheres.

Plate 12
Solar orb. Painting. Rajasthan. c. 18th century A.D.
These astronomical charts were meant to ascertain the sun's altitude
and zenith distance and its declination; to find the declination of a
planet or star; to find the degrees of azimuth of a planet or star to
determine celestial latitudes and longitudes; position during eclipse, etc.
A common practice among astronomers has been to fix on some
epoch, from which, as from a radix, to compute the planetary motions.
The ancient Hindus count back to that point in time when these
motions must have been in conjunction with Mesha or Aries and
supposed it to be the beginning of creation. This would have been
a moderate amount of years compared with the enormous periods of
time mentioned in the different Sanskrit texts; but, having discovered
a slow motion of the modes and apsides also, they found it would
require a length of time corresponding with 1,955,884,890 years then
expired, and 2,304,115,110 years before they would return to the
same point, thus forming together a *kalpa* and assigned as one day
of Brahma. After connecting the four *yugas*, Satya, Treta, Dwapar and
Kali, the whole duration of a Kalpa comes to 4,320,000,000 years.

विद्रुमाक्रूपरे॥९॥

अथक्रांक्रमज्ञानार्थचक्रं												
मेष	वृष:	मिथु	कर्क	सिंह	कंया	तुला	वृश्चि	धन	मक	कुंभ	मीन	रात्रि
था:	अपा	नाश	सुखे	मान	व्यति	स्त्री	लो	चिंता	व्यथा	श्री:	क्षति	
तः	यः			नाश	पीडा		ल्य					

मोहेचंड्रबिंबं

म

ति

गतेर्वचबिंड

सूर्यबिंबं

उ

प

वा

ने

स्थरेचंड्रबिंबं

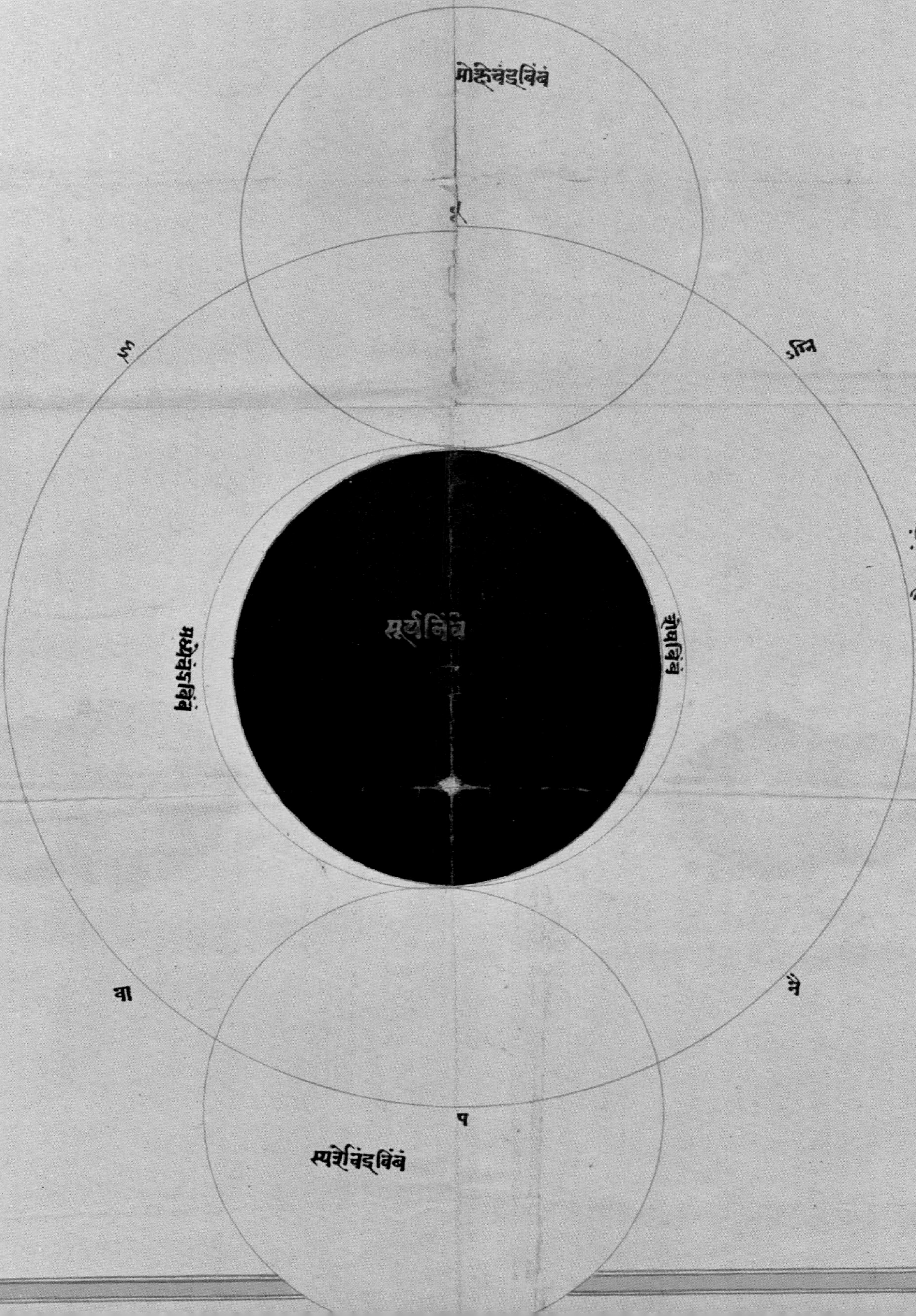

Plate 13
Lunar orb. Painting. Rajasthan. c. 18th century A.D.
The moon does not move exactly in the ecliptic, but in a circle
slightly inclined to it. The points where this path cuts are called
nodes. In ancient astronomy, Rahu and Ketu are the ascending and
descending nodes, and they are also identified with certain planets,
comets, meteors and constellations.

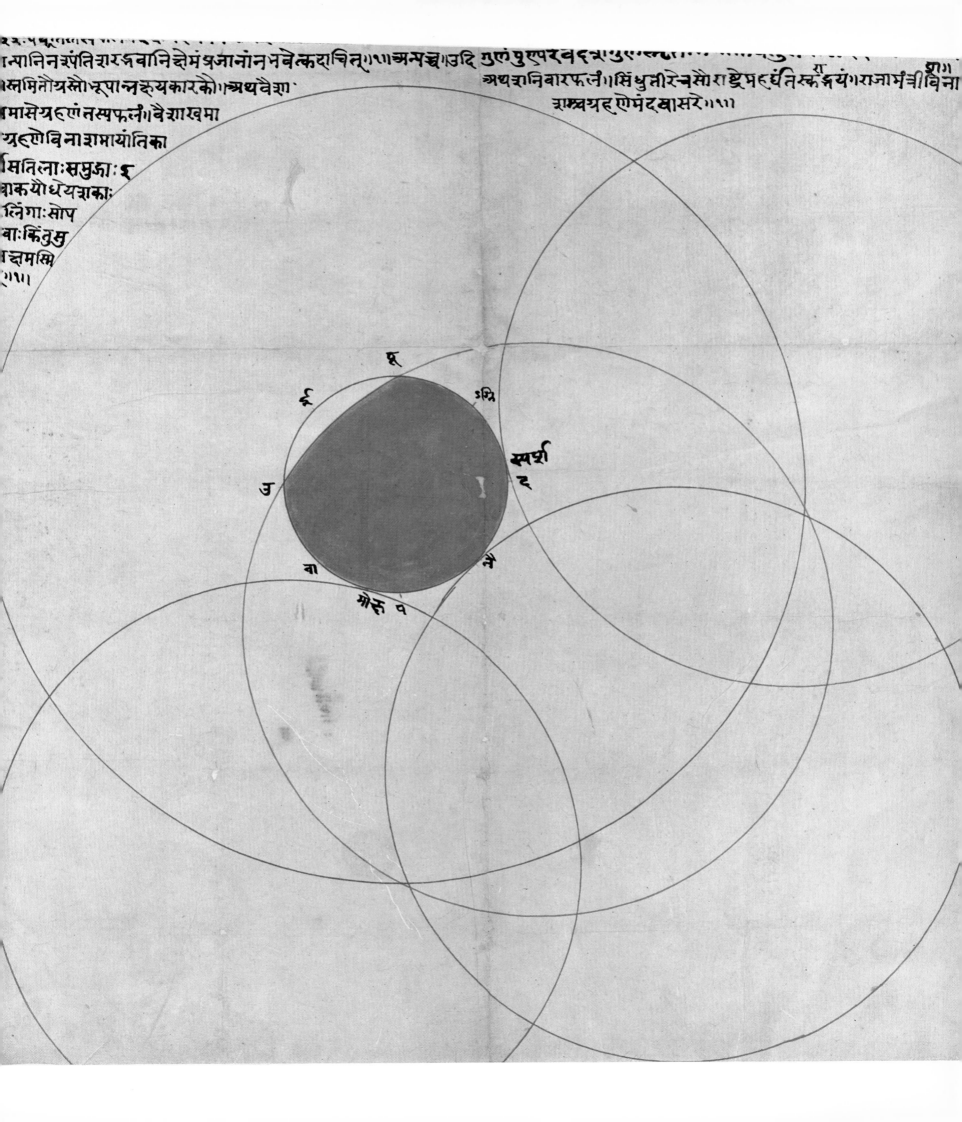

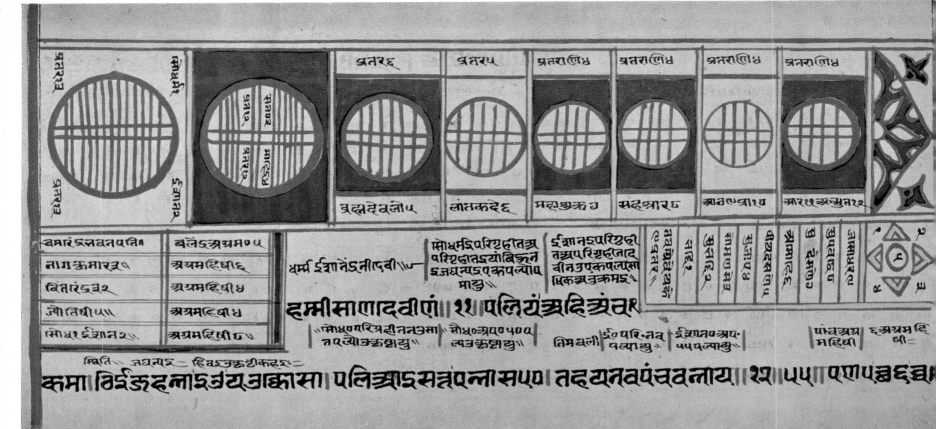

Plate 14
Loka. Painting. Gujarat. c. 1600 A.D. From Sangrahanisutra Ms.
One of the twenty-one *lokas* representing the universe with seven
divisions known as Sapta-lokas which contain different atmospheric
and terrestrial spheres.

Plate 15
Chandra Mandala. Painting. Rajasthan. c. 18th century A.D.
Early Indian astronomy was to a large extent based on astrology,
and the term *jyotisha* covered both. The first methodical presentation
of the subject is found in the Siddhantas, the earliest Hindu treatises
on astronomy and mathematics.

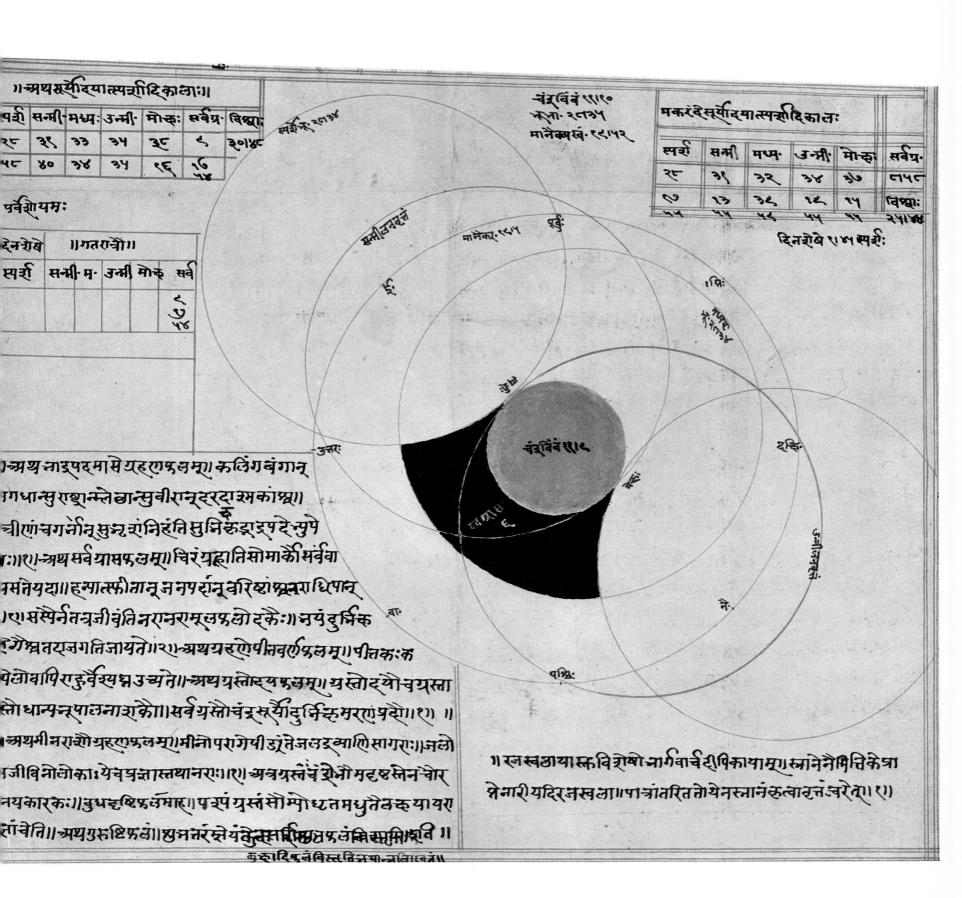

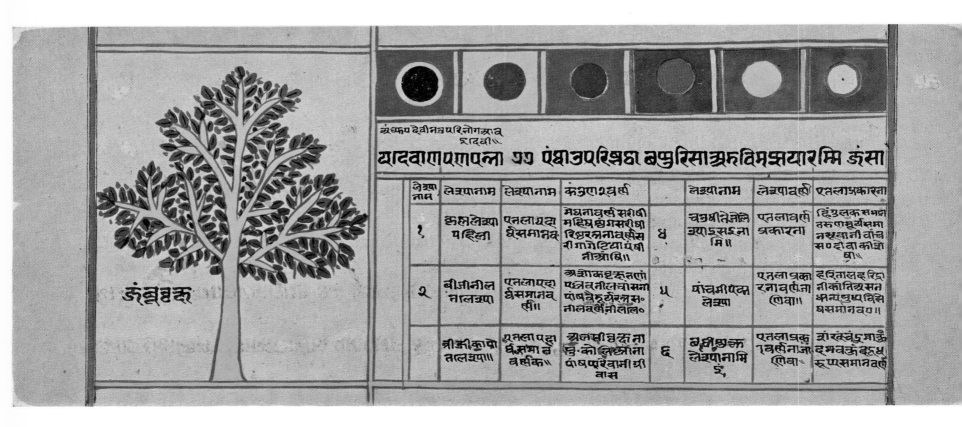

Plate 16
Jambubriksha. Painting. Gujarat. c. 16th century A.D. From an
illuminated Ms.
Jambubriksha, the life-tree, is the radiant manifestation of energy.
The visible universe is the panorama of reflected images of forms
created and produced by light.

Plate 17
Cosmological chart. Painting. Gujarat. c. 16th century A.D. From
a Sangrahanisutra Ms.
Loka, universe: It pervades the entire system with its divisions and
sub-divisions of atmospheric and terrestrial spheres. Aloka the
non-universe space which sustains the Lokas, is represented by red
colour.

All forces of the cosmos are expressions of Prana; it is the sum total of all primal energies. The centrifugal solar energies symbolize conscious awareness while the centripetal lunar energies symbolize the forces of the subconscious mind. These forces flew through the human body as psychic energies along the two main channels, the white-coloured lunar Ida-nadi, the subtle nerve on the left and the red-coloured solar Pingala-nadi on the right. They move in opposite directions around Sushumna-nadi, the fire-coloured middle subtle nerve in the perinium.

These two nerves finally unite with the Sushumna between the eyebrows.

The integral solar and lunar energies are then sublimated and raised from centre to centre until they reach the Sahasrara chakra. Prana, the vital air that moves upward and Apana, that which has a downward motion, are the two important functions of the body. The yogi arrests the separate functions of Ida and Pingala, uniting them with Su-shumna, to be held there by a mudra known as Kumbhaka. Thus the mind of the aspirant becomes stilled, his breath is suspended, his senses are controlled and he achieves the ultimate goal of samadhi.

There is a very close relation between the motion of vital airs, the mind and seminal energy. The relation is so intimate that to arrest any one stops the course of the other two. Tantra sadhana (spiritual discipline) is performed within the subtle body, thereby penetrating psychic zones and activating the depths of the unconscious that lie dormant in the uninitiated. "Man cannot persist long in a conscious state", wrote Goethe, "he must throw himself back into the unconscious, for his root lives there."

Every individual's respiratory cycle reacts dynamically upon the latent Kundalini; this occurs on an average of 21,600 times a day, that is, more or less equal to the individual's number of breaths. However, for the majority of people these breaths are both shallow and fast, filling the lungs to only a fraction of their capacity. Under the circumstances, the current of energy flowing downward to strike at the Kundalini is inadequate to awaken her.

The primary aims of the breathing technique are to force Prana, the upward breath, to flow downward and to strike the latent Kundalini, while simultaneously causing the Apana, a downward breath, to rise. By reversing their usual directions and uniting them at the navel chakra (Manipura), great psychic heat is generated, indicating that the Kundalini is in ascent and has entered Sushumna. She is thus gaining momentum, ready to unite with Siva in the Sahasrara chakra.

All impulse, all function and enjoyment become Siva-Sakti. What on the cosmic plane is fusion of polarities is, on the biological level, sexual union. The yogi and the yogini metamorphose the sex urge into energy until nothing remains of the gross or sensual in the total reconciliation of flesh and spirit. This integration is essential to experience the fullness of life.

Through Tantra asana, sex liberates us from sex and we are freed to a plane of cosmic awareness. The asana itself is a means for the expression of pure joy (ananda) in which the worshipper realizes that all the elements and forces of the universe are within him.

This power can be activated and transmuted into a conscious reality by the practice of Tantra asana. Correct application is most important, for only when the body is perfectly attuned can it experience and sustain the full intensity of this cosmic state. Rather than subdue, Tantra teaches us to realize and harness the potential of the senses. Sexual instinct, an all-pervading urge, is the physical basis of creation and of mankind's evolution. Sex is the cosmic union of opposites from which everything and every being arises. Its importance demands its fulfilment.

The Tantras emphasize that the difference between the inorganic, vital, and mental phenomena is one of degree, not of kind; in the world of diverse objects, there are varying degrees of manifestation of consciousness. In each grain of sand the universe awaits us.

On the physical plane, asana is a fixation on a single point, dharana; and just a concentration on one object puts an end to the digressions of the mind, so asana ends the body's mobility by reducing a number of positions to a single archetype.

The psychic counterpart of this bodily intimacy is a fusion of minds—if no effort is made to induce orgasm by genital friction, the sexual interpenetration creates a psychic interchange. The union itself is great liberation and it is this which becomes cosmic awareness, not the physical act of sexual intercourse known by the gross body.

When the sex energy leaves its customary seat in the upward move to a higher plane, it becomes pure energy. In ordinary life, the highest intensity of pleasure is derived from sexual gratification. But there is a wide dichotomy between this momentary gross pleasure and the bliss of union. The state of post-coitus depression that often follows partial sexual gratification is in sharp contrast to the ecstasy realized through Tantric sadhana.

The Tantric ritual.

The ritual is performed with a partner of the opposite sex. She is considered to be the embodiment of Sakti, the active female principle. Whenever the female principle is found in the living being, we have the potential of the cosmos. Devi and all her attributes are in She. As Tantra says, "Whenever one sees the feet of a woman, one should worship her in one's soul as one does a guru."

It is ideal to have initiation from a Bhairavi (a female guru). This powerful act can only be performed when the guru feels that the disciple is prepared. Otherwise, the path is dangerous, for everything depends on the purity of body, mind and soul. Moreover, the guru knows lakshanas or bodily signs of recognition, indicating which adept is best for a certain rite and also what kind of meditation will yield proper results for a particular aspirant. It requires a long process of preparation and a science has been built up for centuries in India using practical psycho-physical steps to reach the goal. The road to liberation is recognition, to learn that there is no being or object in the cosmos from which we stand apart.

A Tantric can adopt any woman for his asana, no matter in which relation she stands to him, for all human relationships, according to Tantra, are mere thought-constructions. The female participant is called Jnanamudra (the woman of knowledge) or the Maha-mudra (the great woman). The preferred are the washer-maid (Rajakini), the Doma-girl (Domni), or Nartaki (the dancing girl)—those whose essence makes them archetypal of Jung's anima. Ritualistic sexual union is also performed with saha-dharmini (one's own consort), as well as with a woman who is another man's wife (parakiya). Yuvati (young woman). Taruni (damsel), Shodashi (sixteen-year-old girl), or Kumari (virgin) is generally installed as the image of Devi and is worshipped accordingly.

From whatever quarter she comes, the female must meet certain requirements as to appearance and physical condition. She must be in good health, possess a body free of physical defects, have lotus-eyes, full breasts, soft skin, slender waist, fine neck, prominent mons veneris and lustrous hair. The sight of such radiant beauty stimulates all the endocrine glands just as rays of light penetrate the eyes, exciting the anterior pituitary. As electro-magnetic waves act on the male and female, the phallus is enticed into the yoni (vulva).

The yogi must also be in excellent physical condition, with an alert, erect spine. First he must undergo preliminary observances, external and internal purifications and then meditation; through this discipline, all impurities are systematically removed. He must train himself to regard the yogini as a goddess, performing sexual union with her according to traditional rites—otherwise there will be bondage.

The acts of bathing, dressing, sitting for worship, the offering of garlands, incense, foodstuffs, these acts and others are performed in a spirit of total surrender. Here the guru explains the esoteric processes of Tantra sadhana—the means to control the downward tendency of sexual energy and redirect it upward through the strength of union.

Sexual union is one of the Tantric ways for man and woman to direct all the mind's functions to 'one-pointedness'. This union, because of its high intensity, can fuse their consciousness with that of the cosmos. As the Kundalini rises, bodies lose their physical function, the minds of the participants merge into a state where the worshipper and the worshipped become one. They dissolve their beings into the Absolute, rejoicing in the knowledge of their oneness.

The goal is attained individually or collectively. Each one has to plunge within to find the source, yet not by selfishly seeking a private state of bliss—rather, by finding one's true self in the cosmic essence.

The collective asana acts powerfully upon its participants. They receive vibrations from the ritual which move them in the same direction towards a mutual goal. This group participation not only implies the suspension of personal identification, but also of self-assertion. It makes the aspirants unselfish in outlook, free from all attachment and detachment and able to arouse their latent forces.

The basic Tantric conception of unity in duality is expressed in the 'left-hand' practice or vamachara rite of worship. After initiation, the yogi and his sakti are led to the chakra, a mystic circle, to perform the asana. This practice is known among the Vamacharis (left-hand Tantrics) as the ritual of "pancha-makara", the five M's. The makaras (i.e. the ingredients of the left-hand practice) are mada (wine), mamsa (meat), matsya (fish), mudra (fried grain) and maithuna (ritualistic sexual union). If the relevant instructions are taken literally, then Tantrics call this vamachara or left-hand practice; if they are taken in some metaphorical sense, it is then dakshinachara or right-hand practice.

In the pancha-makara rite, the nude female worshipped is no longer regarded as ordinary flesh and blood but as a goddess, as Sakti. Sexual union between her and the yogi symbolizes non dual-existence. Worship is performed in a circle (Sri-chakra, Bhairavi-chakra, Siddha-chakra or Kala-chakra) where an equal number of men and women, without distinction of status, meet during midnight hours in the chosen place in the presence of a guru. Importance is given to the choice of the female consort because as Sakti, she embodies the fundamental forces of the cosmos.

Immediately prior to the sadhana, both partners undergo various physical and mental purifications. Sakti is then liberally and softly massaged with scented oil—jasmine for her hands, keora for the neck and cheeks, champa and hina for breasts, spikenard for the hair, musk for mons veneris, sandalwood for the thighs and saffron or khus for the feet. The primary aim of using certain scents is to stimulate the Muladhara region, which being on the earth plane, is directly related to the sense of smell. Finally, sakti is given a vermilion dot between her brows to mark the place of an opening third eye; in addition, a line is drawn with the vermilion paste from her pubis upward to the bindu-point, indicating the path of the ascending force.

Strict Tantric tradition recognizes only one day each month when the performance of ritual sexual union is proper—the fifth, eighth or fifteenth day of the dark fortnight following the cessation of the sakti's menstrual flow. The menstrual days are also used by the Tantrics following the left-path, as they consider that menstrual blood is not only invigorating but also sedative. It is known that the menstrual discharge is not only composed chiefly of blood potent with ova-energy but also contains other properties, together with a large amount of estrogenic substances (arsenic, lecithin and cholesterol).

The asana practice should begin at a certain propitious time, as nature's influence and planetary pressure have their reflexes in the 'seasons of the body'. The place where the sadhana is to occur is either naturally pure like the river bank, silent forest and mountain top or one duly purified with aspersions. The temperature level must allow partners to remain completely naked for a long period.

When the sadhaka approaches his sakti, now a goddess, to worship her, each ritual embrace, each touch and contact has a symbolic meaning. Reciting mantras, he purifies the five elements of the gross body, known as Bhuta-suddhi, using both japa (repetition of mantras) and ajapajapa (effortless and ceaseless vibration of the sound along with inhalation and exhalation). He then offers honey and other ingredients, sprinkles water, makes ritual fire and other acts of preparation. This is part of nyasa, the process of charging different bodily organs through touch. By transforming his thought process, the Tantric sadhaka is born anew and thus his identity is united with that of his sakti—'aham devi nanyosmi' (I am the goddess, none else).

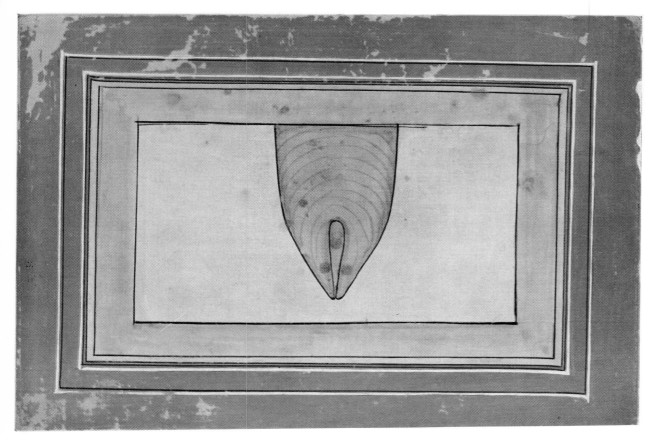

Plate 18
Lunar mansion, Bharani. Painting. Rajasthan. c. 18th century A.D. Bharani is one of the lunar mansions representing yoni with three stars similar to the verse of the Ratnamala. In another Sanskrit text with figures of the same constellations, though calculations vary, the mathematical astronomers allow thirteen *ansas* and one-third, or thirteen degrees twenty minutes to each of the twenty-seven lunar stations known as *nakshatras*. The number of stars in each of the twenty-seven asterisms is described as "three, three, six; five, three, one; four, three, five; five, two, two; five, one, one; four, four, three; eleven, four and three; three, four, one hundred; two, two, thirty-two. Thus have the stars of the lunar constellations, in the order that they appear, been numbered by the wise."

Plate 19 →

← Plate 19
Astronomical Computation. Painting. Kangra, Himachal Pradesh.
c. 18th century A.D.
The Hindu system assumes that at the beginning of creation, when
the planetary motions began, a line drawn from the equinoctial point
Lanka through the centre of the earth world, if continued, have
passed through the centre of the sun and planets to the first star in
Aries; their mean longitude for any determined time afterwards may
be computed. As the revolutions a planet makes in any cycle are in
proportion to the number of days composing it, so are the days given
to its motion in that time; and even revolutions being rejected,
the faction, if any, shows its mean longitude at midnight under their
first meridian of Lanka: for places east or west of that meridian a
proportional allowance is made for the difference of longitude on
the earth's surface, called in Sanskrit the Deshantara. The positions
of the apsides and nodes are computed in the same manner.
As the solar months in a Yug, 51,840,000, are to the intercalary lunar
months in that cycle, 1,593,336, so are the solar months 23,470,618,687,
to the corresponding intercalary lunar months 721,384,677; which
added together, give 24,192,003,364 lunations.
This number multiplied by thirty produces 725,760,100,920 *tithis*,
or lunar days, from the creation to the new moon in Kartic to which
add fourteen *tithis* for the same (to the *Purnimah tithis* in that month
725,760,100,934).
Then, as the number of *tithis* in a Yug, 1,603,000,080, is to their
difference exceeding the mean solar days in that cycle 25,082,252 so
are 725,760,100,920 *tithis*, to their excess in number over the solar
days 11,356,017,987, which subtracted, leaves 714,404,082,947, as the
number of mean solar days from the creation, or when the planetary
motions began, to a point of time when it will be midnight under the
first meridian of Lanka, and near the time of full moon in Kartic.

Plate 20
Jambu-dvipa. Painting. Rajasthan. c. 18th century A.D.
The position of Jambu-dvipa in relation to the universe forms an
integral part of Tantric and Pauranic cosmology. The cardinal centre
of the whole cosmographical conception is the symbolical Mount
Meru around which stands the region of Ilavrita. Beyond Ilavrita lies
Jambu-dvipa which is surrounded by a number of concentric circles
showing the symbols of life. Beyond the outermost circle lies the
sphere of Lokaloka (world no-world), which divides the visible
world from the invisible.

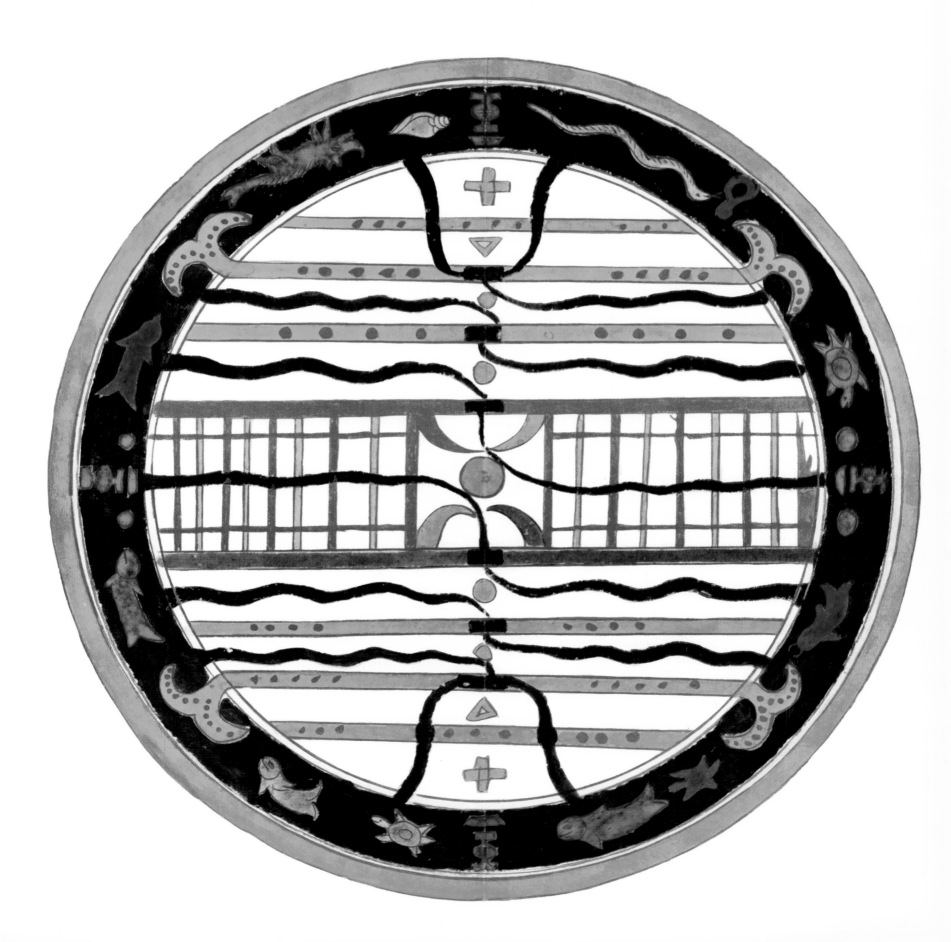

Plate 21
Mahalinga Mandala. Painting. Rajasthan. c. 18th century A.D.
Siva-linga, the all pervading space, symbolizes a cosmic form. There
are, it is believed, twelve genuine *jyotir-lingas*, or "effulgent lingas"
in India. The sacred lingas are sometimes named after the places
where they are situated or are given separate distinctive names,
often descriptive variations of the name of Siva. The name Siva, the
Red One, is related to the Tamil word for "red", as the name Rudra
also is synonymous with red. Siva is said to have 1008 names or
epithets, of which Nandikeshara, Bamadeva, Mahakal, Rudra,
Bhairava, Aghora, are given in this mandala.

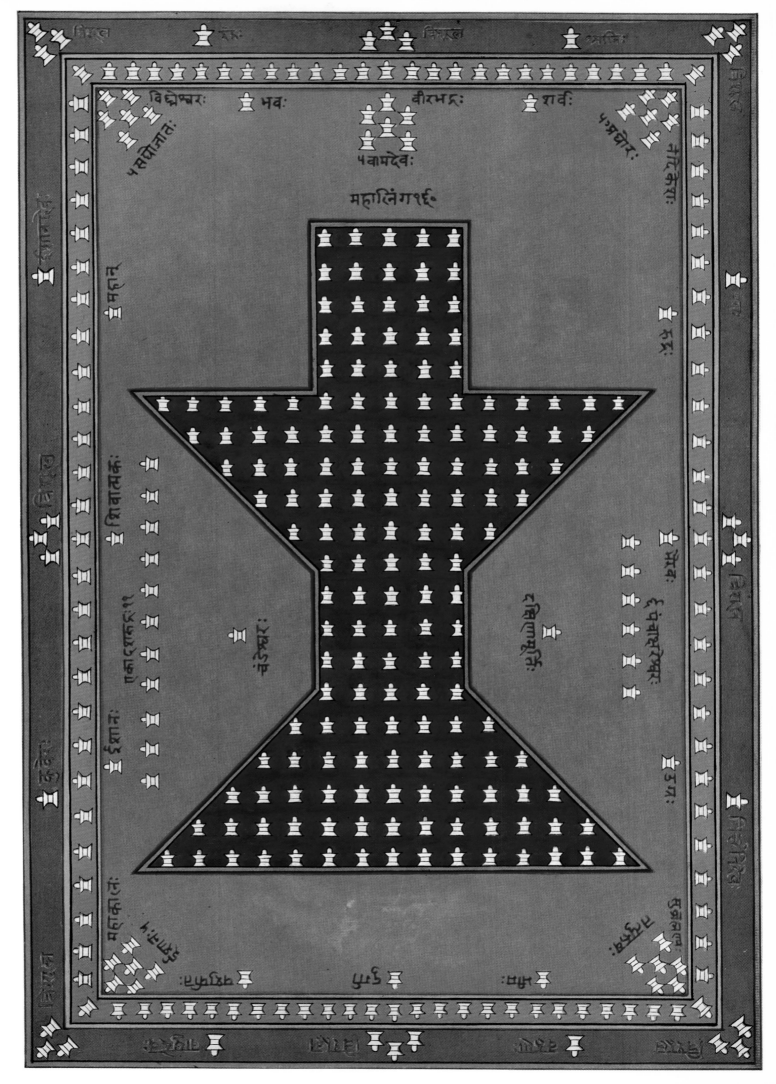

Plates 22–24
Brahmanda, Stone. Contemporary expression of ageless traditional form. The First Cause formed the Hiranya-garbha or "golden womb", a golden cosmic egg, which floated upon the surface of the primeval waters. The egg then divided itself into two parts forming the twenty-one regions of the cosmos. Some schools of Hindu philosophy postulate the existence of primeval matter (*prakriti*) from which the world was made or evolved. The Prapancasara Tantra states that Prakriti as sound pervades the Brahmanda. This Sound, or Sabda, generates vibration which evolves, sustains and destroys every form.

Plate 25
Sahasradala (detail). From an illuminated Ms. Nepal. c. 1760 A.D. Bharat Kala Bhavan, Banaras.
The symbolic lotus with the thousand petals (*sahasradala*) located just above the crown of the head is said to be the halo of the cerebral cortex. When Kundalini rises from the cardinal circle (Muladhara chakra) piercing through the other five chakras in the human body, she ultimately unites with her Purusha in the Sahasrara; thus ends all duality. The red triangle represents the female or active force and white the male or static element.

Plate 26

Sambhu Yantra. From an illuminated Ms. Painting. Nepal. c. 1760 A.D. Bharat Kala Bhavan, Banaras.

The duality that persists in this yantra manifests itself as Siva-Sakti, or Purusha and Prakriti, as the balance of form and energy. This character is indicated by white and red bindus symbolizing the male and female essence. The *bindu* carries within itself the seeds of the future, its multiple potentialities, symbolically represented by the combination of white and red half circles. The *bindu* contains within itself the two "poles" (zero and infinity). Its inherent energy is the *alaya-vijnana* or *bindu* containing all dualities and all polarities, subject and object, beginning and end, within or without, male and female. But for the actual creative process, the *bindu* must evolve beyond duality to the *trikona*—the triangle, the first rectilinear figure defining dimension.

Plate 27
Linga-Yoni. Painting. Kangra, Himachal
Pradesh. c. 18th century A.D.
Siva stands for Asabda Brahman, the
unqualified one and Sakti for Sabda
Brahman, the creative impulse in the
cosmic process. Linga, according to
Skanda Purana, is the name for space in
which the whole universe is in the
process of formation and dissolution.
Siva-linga, the all-pervading space,
symbolizes a cosmic form. Gouri-patta
represents *adya-sakti*, the energy quanta:
Mahamaya, the power of manifestation;
Yoni, the primal root or source of
objectivation. Hence Linga-Yoni is
the embodiment of both inaction and
action.

50 Plate 28

Siva-Linga. Polished stone. Gudimallam, Tamil Nadu. First century B.C. Photograph: Archaeological Survey of India.

Five feet in height, the Siva-linga with a figure of Siva carved on its lower portion, is a cosmic form pervading the whole universe and also present in the human body in the Muladhara chakra as the Svayambhu linga, encircled by Kundalini Sakti which is the dormant vital energy.

Plate 29
Chaitanya's Khunti. Brass. Nabadwip, West Bengal. c. 17th century A.D.
Flagstaff representing Lord Chaitanya generally carried by devotees of the Vaishnava sects at the time of devotional processions *(nagar-kirtans)*.

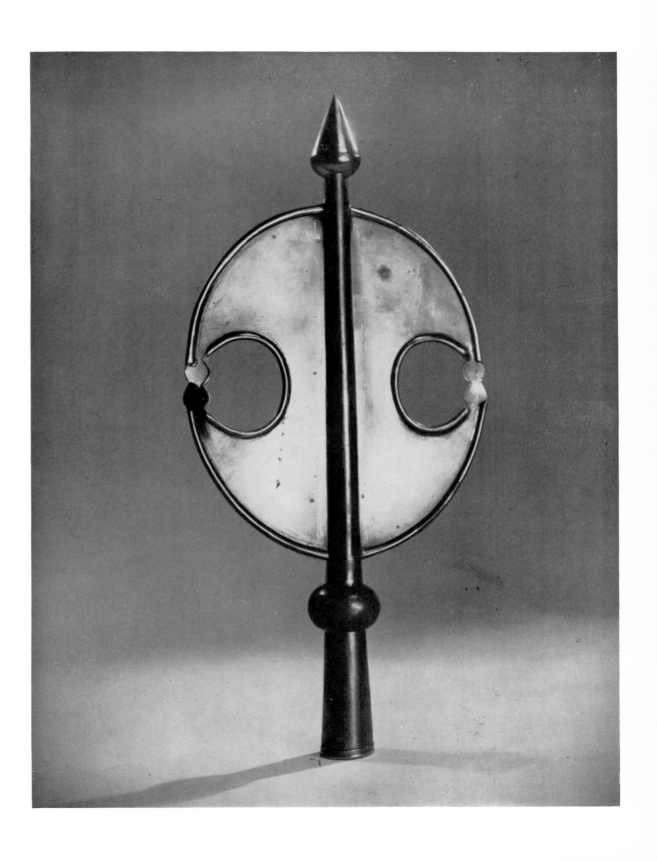

Ekapada. Stone. Chausatti Yogini Temple. Hirapur, Orissa. c. 11th century A.D.
Photograph: Archaeological Survey of India.
The unification of Siva and Vishnu is represented as Aja Ekapada (one-footed deity) with
urdhalinga, the erect phallus which signifies that he is consubstantial with the penetrating
power of the universe.

Plate 31

Hari-Hara. Painting. Basholi, Jammu-Kashmir. c. 17th century A.D. In the ritual of Panchayatana, Vishnu (Hari), the preserver, merges with Siva (Hara), the destroyer, to symbolize the eternal cycle of birth and rebirth.

Plate 32
Hari-Hara Mandala. Painting. Rajasthan. c. 18th century A.D.
The underlying idea of merging of Hari with Hara, Vishnu with Siva, accompanied by the knowledge of Brahma, is to find perfect synthesis. This is symbolized by a square *bindu* in the centre surrounded by eighty-four yogini power-fields which sustain the different regions.

Plate 33
Vishnu-padas. Painting. Rajasthan. c. 18th century A.D.
The feet of Vishnu symbolize the unity of the entire universe. All the elements of the universe are represented by various auspicious signs indicating many aspects of the Ultimate One. As fundamentally all things are one since they are only fragments of the Supreme Unity, they are to be regarded as symbols or emblems of a higher reality.

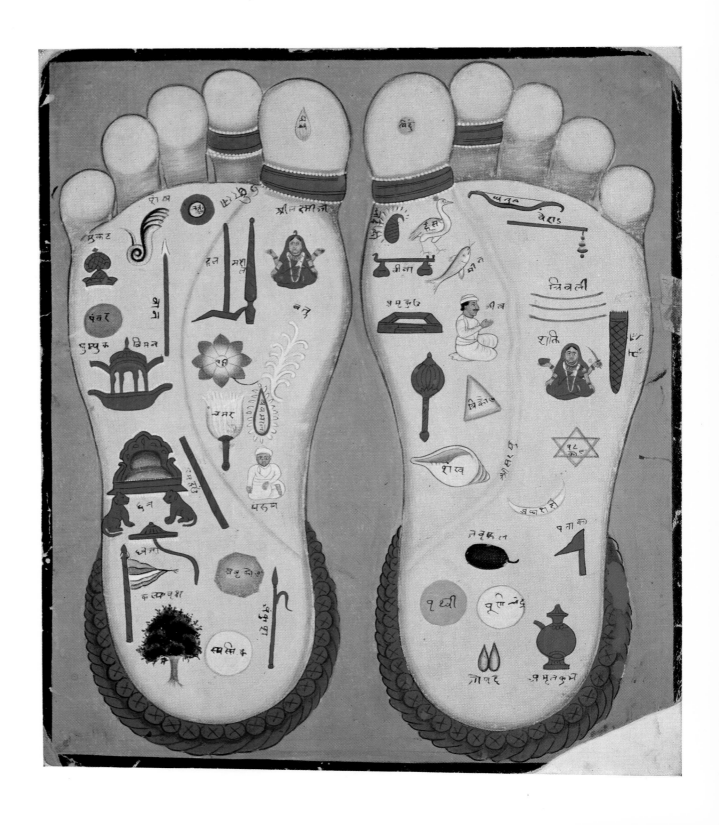

55

Plate 34
Nagalingan. Drawing. Rajasthan. Contemporary expression
of ageless traditional form. Photograph: Archaeological Survey
of India.
This type of yantra, commonly known as *paglya* is a characteristic
feature of *mandana* (mandala?) drawings. There is an intimate
connection between cosmic creation and the primal urge of man
and woman, symbolized here by serpent power. The differences
between the macrocosm and the microcosm are resolved through
union.

Plate 35
Ardhanarisvara. Painting. Kangra, Himachal Pradesh.
c. 18th century A.D.
This composite figure of Siva and Parvati as half male
and half female indicates that male and female elements
are balanced in both of them. Full emancipation is
dependent upon our realization of this fact.

Plate 36
Vishnu's Anantasayana. Painting. Kangra, Himachal Pradesh.
c. 18th century A.D.
At the end of the *maha-pralaya* or universal dissolution, Vishnu,
resting on the serpent-bed, Ananta or Adishesha, is conceived as the
Infinite Being resting in a state of cosmic slumber *(yoga-nidra)*. On the
lotus sprung from the navel of Vishnu is seated Brahma, the creator,
encountering the two destructive forces Madhu and Kaitabha in the
chaotic waters of the dissolved cosmos, while Mahadevi endowed
with all the powers *(sakti)*, is assuming a form indicating that the
dissolution of the cosmos is in fact the beginning of its creation.

Mantras uttered during the rite are so designed as to create appropriate vibrations within a psychic field. The yogi utters bija-mantras, seed-syllables of one-pointed thought activity, directing them towards different parts of both his and his sakti's body. During all these processes, he meditates on and repeats the Sanskrit mantras: " om ananda-bhairavyai namah" (salutation to ananda bhairavi), or "Om, Hrim, Kling, Kandarpa svaha; Om, Hrim, Krom, svaha." The male and female psyches are always attuned to the vibrations a powerful mantra can create. The seat is first sanctified with mantras (asana-suddhi) and then the devotees take their seats, which are made of kusa grass with a deer skin or a raw-wool cloth on top. If Sakti wraps herself around her partner like a vine, this rite is known as lata-sadhana. But most frequently, the female adept sits astride the male yogi, while he himself takes one of the traditional postures.

The entire rite is carried out in dim light, the best kind of illumination being a castor oil lamp which produces a violet hue. At the time of union, this lamp is positioned so that its rays fall directly upon the Muladhara region of the sakti. It is believed that violet light stimulates the female sex glands, whereas red light activates those of the male.

Light and sound play an important part in the panchamakara rite. In purifying themselves, the adepts make use of different colours. For example, the sadhaka wears red cloth of raw-wool, provided the material is a non-conductor, the shade being close to that of the hibiscus (Jaba), the symbolic colour of Tantra, whereas sakti wraps herself in thin silk of a violet or pink colour. The cosmic rays that strike the body are incorporated within by the process of Pranayama. Corresponding vibrations are set up, as each breath with its own characteristic colour rays penetrates the various chakras, being absorbed and when rediffused through chromatic colour breathing.

During sexual union, the minds of the participants are withdrawn from the physical environment as they identify themselves completely with urge for freedom. The retention of sexual energy increases inner pressure, thus transmuting the sex forces into a potency so tremendous that the psychic current is liberated. Individual identity is lost in open intuitive contact. At this moment, body and soul become one as physical pleasure is transformed into the subtle inexpressible joy of liberation.

Sexual energy is controlled through Hatha-yoga and other processes called mudra, bandha, asana and pranayama. These control the expansion and contraction of the pelvic region, the same muscles and nerves often being associated with breath-control. Among the mudras, the most important are the Vajroli, Sahajoli and Amoroli; others include the Khechari-mudra, the Maha-mudra, the Asvani-mudra, the Yoni-mudra. The latter is required in Siddhasana when the aspirant's craving for a return to the womb (yoni), the source of origin, develops great erectile and seminal power which is necessary for a prolonged asana. The proper practice of these mudras and asanas ensures retention of sexual energy in both partners. If by chance the orgasm occurs, the fluids must be withdrawn into the bodies by the Vajroli-mudra. Through the bandhas, contraction of the pelvic region is also possible, the most effective being the Uddiyana-bandha, Mula-bandha and Maha-vedha.

This triple control—breath, power over seminal ejaculation and mental digressions—is effected simultaneously, with the whole force of esoteric meditation directed towards this end. Aspirants must retain their sexual energy, because the indiscriminate discharge of the vital fluids in both male and female is a waste of the psychic force. Biologically speaking, the average healthy person performs 'three to four thousand' sexual acts in the course of a genital life of 30 to 40 years. If 100 to 200 million spermatozoa are produced daily in the human body, one can see the magnitude of loss which inevitably disturbs the energy equilibrium.

The testes secrete fluids which circulate in the body, adding enormously to man's magnetic and spiritual development. In the female system, the ovaries' secretion is also absorbed, adding to her physical and spiritual well-being. These two vital elements in male and female reciprocally charge one another. The body's richest blood produces the reproductive ingredients in both sexes; from this, an indefinable power, Ojah, is generated in the body. It is said that only 3½ drops of Ojah (élan vital) are stored up during the span of one life and from this, our micro-macrocosm structure draws all substance.

Electro-chemical energy passes between the human bodies during the sexual union. The male genitals are electrical on the exterior and magnetic within, while those of the female are magnetic on the exterior and electrical within. Thus a field is created for the exchange of cosmic force. The psychic currents which flow from body to body do so through invisible conduits, nadis, situated in the subtle body. The guru gives precise instructions to ensure correct flow of vital energies between the embraced bodies.

All human energy is polarized into anabolism and katabolism, the one tending to conserve and the other to release. The same forces exist in Tantra sadhana, making birth, sex and death mere human manifestations of a cosmic pattern in which all happenings are but a reflection. The bisexual potential exists in equal male-female (M/F) ratios in the reproduction protoplasm. Visually, it has been depicted as the form of Ardhanarisvara (Siva-Parvati), male and female attributes shown as part of the same body, hermaphroditically joined. The idea that masculinity and feminity are two separate factors is as illusory as that of the duality of body and soul.

One whose sexual energy is directed upwards is known as Urdhareta, also meaning a person who has completely overcome all carnal desires. To be an Urdhareta is not merely to control the emission of gross semen but also to prevent its formation as such and ultimately to be able to absorb it into the system.

It is said that the release of sexual energy gradually spreads throughout the entire body. In the same way, the psycho-sexual force generated by a concentrated asana can produce extraordinary phenomena within the body; such an example is the human aura. After sexual union, a kind of radiation takes hold of the personality—an egg-shaped nebula surrounds the body on all sides for a distance of two to three feet. It is a universal form, the same as the foetus and brahmanda.

The Tantrics often practice asana on a cremation ground, a rite known as savasana. Meditation on certain kinds of corpses stresses the truth of transcience; consequently, such a place is ideal for meditation. Thus the yogi's heart itself becomes a cremation ground—pride and selfishness, status and role, name and form are all burnt to ashes. Since cremation grounds and midnight hours are best for undisturbed meditation, an explosion of psychic potential occurs. The atmosphere is charged with powers that can frighten the aspirant. He must first overcome the terrifying images and temptations that confront him before an awareness of tranquillity can be established.

Asana is actually a step by step dissolution of the gross into subtle elements, a process of gradual involution whereby the body is identified with its elementary sources; earth is associated with the sense of smell, water with taste, fire with vision, air with touch, ether with sound. These five elements are merged one by one into their sources, with the potentials of the energies (tanmatras); and ultimately the ego (ahamkara) is dissolved into mahat, the great one, 'the cognitive totum of the cosmos', and this into Sakti or Prakriti (the inscrutable primal Energy-Matter); finally Sakti is merged with Siva or Purusha, the Pure Consciousness. This consciousness is constantly coming down in a shower on human beings, but because of cosmic bombardment, it is immediately transformed and diffused throughout the body. In reuniting Siva-Sakti, the adept can reach out and enjoy the 'nectar' falling from the Sahasrara chakra, 'the centre of communication directly between the individual being and the infinite consciousness above' (Sri Aurobindo).

● ●

Such is the creative mystery in which we seek to understand the hidden in the cosmos and the human soul. It is not by ceasing to act that we can embrace all levels of being, but rather by purifying all our acts. Nothing is excluded, even the sexual impulse itself is ready to be harmonized and this transformation is spiritual realization.

Within this awareness is the anti-thesis of the desire to possess. So the Goddess Basholi said to Chandidasa, the greatest exponent of Padavali songs in fifteenth-century Bengal: "the woman you love, you must not possess." The Brahmin rebel Chandidasa had dared to love Rami, the washer-maid. The Sahaja and Baul sects (offshoots of Tantra in Bengal) reflect this same freedom and stress on the importance of love. The word 'Sahaja' means that which is natural and spontaneous.

Love is the cosmic force of compassion expressed through the male and female and therefore, through sexual union, we can realize Pure Love. As the two become one, like complement and essence, they experience Sahaja bliss, where love is the sublime in human beings. The tremendous force of inflowing love is manifest on all scales, from the atoms to the galaxies. So Swami Vivekananda says: "Love opens the most impossible gates, love is the gate to all the secrets of the universe." Until we live freely, we cannot transcend the worldly state of being. Sahaja, the natural way, denies suppression and its resulting strain; instead, man should take the easiest path along which his own nature leads him. In the same way, this emphasis explains the Sahaja and Baul view that marriage is a corrupt institution, in that it preserves that bondage against which we inwardly rebel. But Tantric union is in tune with the cosmos—here there is love for all things and all beings.

All that remains is an insatiable desire for unity, only a lover and a loved. This totality is called samarasa. Here the male and female return to the primal condition of Siva-Sakti. There is no separation, only the body moving without knowing itself in motion, complete surrender of the human being to the Absolute. All is One.

From bliss proceeds the cosmos, it is sustained in bliss and dissolved in bliss.

Plate 37
Brahma-loka. Painting. Rajasthan, c. 1700 A.D.
The Brahmanda or "egg of Brahma" comprises the whole cosmos and contains the twenty-one zones called lokas, "locality" arranged in stratas known as the tri-lokas, three worlds—Sattva (conscience-superior world), Rajas (phenomenal world) and Tamas (netherworld). The figure in centre is Brahma, the creator seated in the eight petals of the yellow lotus. The blue figure above the lotus is that of Vishnu, the preserver. In front of Vishnu is Prakriti, the nature and the blue figure directly below the lotus petals is Siva, the destroyer. Sakti, the cosmic energy is seated right in front of Siva. The boar-headed figure is Varah one of the incarnations of Vishnu, who saves the world from extinction. And Indra, the king of Heavens is right opposite Varah. The first five inner circles (beginning with blue colour) intercepting the seven spokes represent different mounts, such as Suvarna (gold), Pushpak (flower), Devanik (abode of Angels), Mount Meru (centre of the earth), Mandrachal (the point where earth touches with the rest of the universe). Colours such as the inner blue circle represent the time element prior to the formation of the earth. While the gold depicts Satayuga (the era of truthfulness). The purple represents Dwaparyuga (period of degradation) and the yellow colour portrays the Tretayuga (third epoch) where the good and evil exist side by side. And the remaining grey depicts the age of darkness. Thus the seven outer circles represent the different colours of the cosmos. Similarly the four elephants (Diggaj) of directions, are keepers of each cardinal points and the chariot with deer depicts Moon (night) while the chariot with seven horses represent the Sun (day). They symbolize the universe and our planetary system.

Plate 38
Bhuvanesvari Yantra. Painting. Rajasthan. c. 18th century A.D.
In this Yantra, the Devi is depicted in her aspect as the controller of the
universe. Devi, as Sati, Uma, Parvati, and Gauri, is spouse of Siva. It was as
Sati that the Devi manifested herself to Siva in the ten forms celebrated in
Tantra Shastra as the *dashamahavidya*—Kali, Bagala, Chhinnamasta, Bhuva-
nesvari, Matangini, Soroshi, Dhumavati, Tripurasundari, Tara and Bhairavi.
These are but some of her endless forms. She exists, too, in all organic and
inorganic things, since the universe, with all its manifestations is, as the
Devi Purana says, but a part of her. The Tantrasara in its hymn to the goddess
says: "Bhuvanesvari, the cause and mother of the world, she whose form is
that of the *sabdabrahman*, and whose substance is 'Bliss'."

Plate 39
Megalithic monument. Stone. Kerala. Photograph: Archaeological
Survey of India.
A huge slab of circular dome mounted on a yoni shaped mound of the
same material with an entrance passage leading to *garbha-griha*,
the womb-chamber foreshadows the concept of linga-yoni in temple
architecture.

Plate 40
Adi-Sakti. Terracotta (Jhunsi). Allahabad Museum, Uttar Pradesh.
c. 2nd century A.D. Photograph: Archaeological Survey of India.
The transcendental influence of Prakriti initiates the process of
creation; the yoni is the primal root or the source of objectivation
and believed to possess a life of its own. The yoni is treated as a
sacred area worthy of reverence, a symbol of cosmic force. It is the
ultimate ground in which the seed of all creation is planted and
nourished. All life generates in the womb and in due course all things
emerge from therein.

Adi-Sakti. Terracotta (Jhunsi). Allahabad Museum, Uttar Pradesh.
c. 2nd century A.D. Photograph: Archaeological Survey of India.

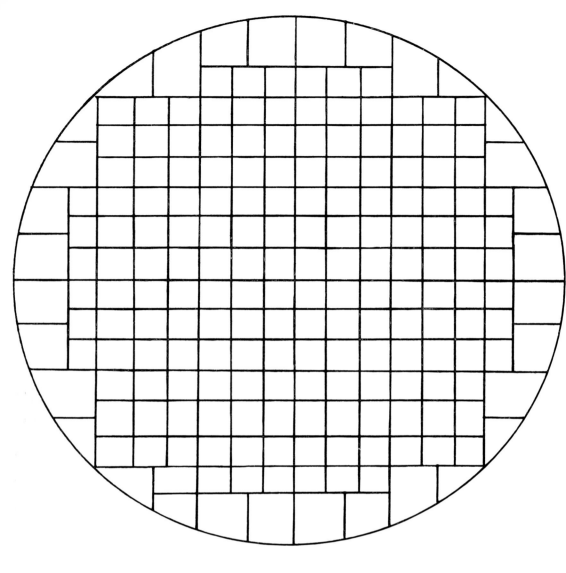

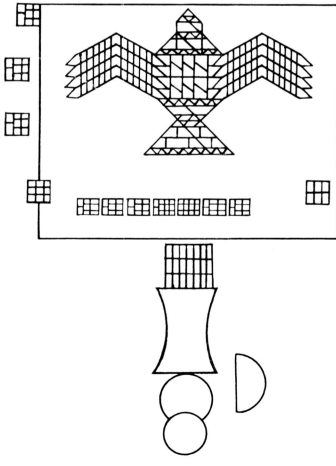

Plate 41
The form of a Vedic (1500 B.C.) geometrical diagram of Ratha
Chakra-vedi (Agni or fire in the shape of a massive wheel). A square is
formed with an area of 7½ square "*purusha*" (the height measure
of a man) and the square is turned into a circle.

Plate 42
Geometrical diagram for a Vedic sacrificial alter called Mahavedi.
The measurements for the alter area, East—24; West—30; Prachi
(eastern horizon)—36. The units of measurement is chosen according
to requirements. The Mahavedi covers an area of 972 units. The
sadas measure 9 cubits by 27 cubits.

Plate 43
Yoni. Brick. Jagatgram. Uttar
Pradesh. c. 3rd century A.D.
Photograph: Archaeological
Survey of India.
During the excavation of the
Asvamedha site, the plan of *soma*
rite performed by some kings of
ancient India in connection with
the horse sacrifice was found. This
brick represents *yoni*. Following
the sacrifice of the horse, the chief
queen lay in the sacrificial pit,
holding the horse's member and
went through the motions of
union with the animal which was
now identified with Prajapati,
"creation's king". It is also
evidenced in some later paintings
that before the animal was sacri-
ficed the chief queen underwent
the same ritual with the living
horse.

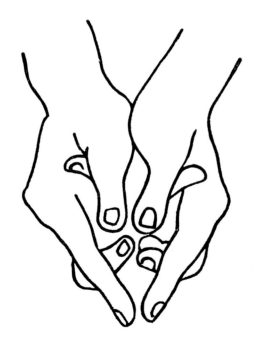

Plate 44
Yoni mudra. Yoni, the womb
source of all things, symbolizes the
feminine organ: the fingers are
brought together to circumscribe
the form with a triangle.

Plate 45
Yoni (detail). Chausatti Yogini Temple. Stone. Bheraghat, Madhya
Pradesh. c. 12th century A.D. Photograph: Archaeological
Survey of India.
The *yoni* under the feet of the Devi, one of the images in the
Chausatti Yogini temple, represents *adya-sakti*, the primal energy.

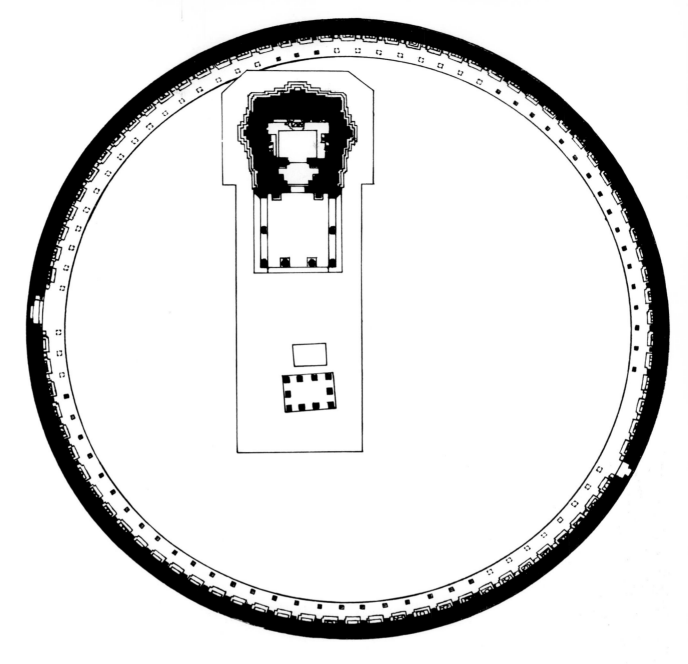

Plate 46
Ground Plan of the Temple of Sixty-four Yoginis (Chausatti Yogini).
Bheraghat, Madhya Pradesh. c. 12th century A.D.
In the chakra (circular worship) a group of male and female
aspirants meet for a performance of ceremonial rite. This circular
type of temple used for tantric ritual has a cosmic significance
symbolically representing the eternal quality of the union of opposites.

रजः

"Divided into two parts, I create"

Devi Bhagavata

Plate 47

Chhinnamasta. Painting. Rajasthan. c. 18th century A.D.

Devi in her destructive and creative aspects signifies apparent dissolution and return to the elements and reconstitution into other forms thus the process of being is an unbroken, infinite one. Within the solar-chakra is the goddess Chhinnamasta, as effulgent as tens of millions of suns together; she is naked, *digambari* (space-clad), full-breasted. But her womb is the sphere of endless creation and dissolution.

Her third eye looks beyond space and time. She is the changeless, limitless primordial power creating the great drama. On the left and right side of the Devi are Dakini and Barnini. Under the Devi's *yogasana* Rati and Kama, the female and male principles, depict transcendence of the phenomenal world and an abolition of all experience of duality.

Plate 48
Rati and Kama. Painting. Kangra, Himachal Pradesh. c. 18th century A.D.
Rati is Kama's sakti representing kinetic energy. Kama is the god of love about whom
it is said in the Vedas: "Desire first arose at the dawn of creation." In the Atharva-Veda,
Kama is known as the creation. They remain in a union of oneness, enjoying that
supreme bliss which is the highest non-duality.

Plate 49
Ritual designs. Painting. Rajasthan. c. 1900 A.D.
Photograph: Archaeological Survey of India.
After the act of *sodhana* or purification by ritual bath,
certain parts of the female body are decorated with
auspicious signs. The *madanadi*, accompanied by
the recitation of mantras, was stimulated and used
for these zones which were regarded as cross-points
of the cosmos and as chakras peculiar to the female
body.

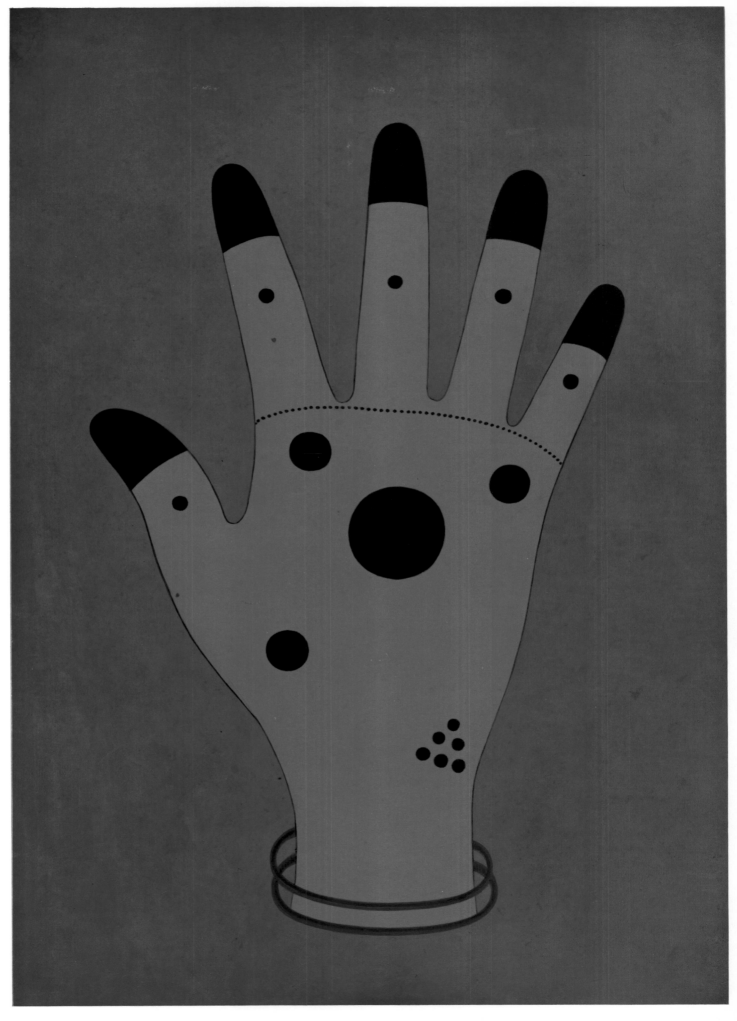

Plate 50
Surasundari. Stone. Khajuraho. Madhya Pradesh.
950–1050 A.D. Photograph: S.L.Vohra.
She is the primordial spirit of manifestation, the
symbol of illusion, *maya*, the desire for creation and
appearance, whose sport is universal-play reflected
in the mirror that she holds. She is one of the Ashta-
Saktis (Eight Energies) who exist in all qualities and
the universe is but her own form. Her *dyana mantra*:
"Om Hring Agaccha Surasundari Svaha."

Plate 51
Stripuja. Stone. Konarak. Orissa. 1240–1280 A.D.
Photograph: Archaeological Survey of India.
Stripuja, female worship, is one of the major rites
in tantric rituals in which the nude female is object
of worship and meditation. By concentration on
matters pertaining to sexo-yogic practices the
psychic centres are believed to be activated and
stimulated till a high degree of enlightenment is
attained.

Plate 52
Matrika Yantra. Painting. Rajasthan. c. 18th century A.D.
The mother is the main bond of union. She is the epitome of energy
and power. Regarded as the active principle of the universe, she is
often conceived of as having greater importance than the male.
She is identified with the Ultimate, since she combines in her person
both the Universal Male and the Universal Female.

Plate 53
Kumari-puja. Stone. Sri Ranga Temple, Tiruchi-
rapalli, Tamil Nadu. c.16th century A.D. Photograph: Archaeological Survey of India.
Kumari-puja, virgin-worship, is one of the most
important tantric rituals in which the nude female
and the yoni are objects of worship and meditation.
A menstruating virgin is also worshipped as
Sodashi. But a girl of prepuberty age from five to
twelve, is said to be the embodiment of the goddess
herself. By means of various rites and rituals she is
transformed into the living image of Sakti. This
discipline is considered extremely perilous if
ignorantly or lustfully performed. Only adepts
who are profoundly initiated can draw psychic
energy from this rite.

Plate 54
Yogini. Stone. Palampet, Ramappa Temple,
Andhra Pradesh. c. 12th century A.D. Photograph:
Archaeological Survey of India.
A male practising yoga disciplines is a yogi, the
female is a yogini. The term yoga has been derived
from the Sanskrit root yuj, "yoke", its aim is to
fuse the human soul *(Jivatman)* in complete unition
with the universal soul *(Paramatman)*. Extensive
yoga practices lead to the attainment of realization
through the arousal of the psychic energy symbolized
by the serpent.

Plate 55

A female figure. Painting. Basholi, Jammu-Kashmir.
c. 17th century A.D.

A female figure illustrating positions of Amritakala, which have to be energised on respective dates of the white and dark halves of the month for successful tantric asanas. The eighteen focal centres in the female body mentioned in Ratirahasya can be excited by the adept when harmonised with the exact location of the *chandrakala* (digits of the moon) on the respective dates of the white as well as the dark halves of the month.

Plate 56

Anointing. Painting. Rajasthan. c. 18th century A.D.

Prior to initiation, a woman undergoes a rite of *abhisheka* or purification of the body with oil and consecrated water in order to gain the right of sitting in sacred asana. To realize the state of absoluteness, a Vamachari, left-hand tantric, conceives of himself as the male deity, and by yogic practices transfigures his partner into the Sakti or his divine female counterpart. The pair then unite in tantric asana.

90 Plate 57
Initiation. Stone. Siva Temple, Ramgarh, Rajasthan. c. 12th
century A.D. Photograph: Archaeological Survey of India.
Before entry is granted into the tantric inner circle an aspirant
goes through various initiation rituals.

Plate 58
Initiation. Painting. Rajasthan. c. 18th century A.D.
Initiation into the tantric inner circle is through the rite of
chakra-puja which is supposed to raise one from the profane to
the sacred state. It is a secret rite by which a person enters the
mysteries of an esoteric order by the guru.

Plate 59
Asana. Terracotta. Harappa, Punjab. c. 3000 B.C. Collection of Antiquities, Safdarjung, New Delhi.
This type of terracotta figurine according to B.B. Lal, Director General of Archaeology in India,
represents the earliest example of asana. The Harappan tradition of yogic practices as represented
in different seals and figures of the Indus Valley was undoubtedly continued throughout subsequent
periods. Dr. B.M. Barua even observes that the phonetic values as suggested in the Tantric code
might correctly be identified with the Indus signs.

Plate 60
Paryankabandha asana. Seal. Mohenjo-daro. c. 2500 B.C. National Museum, New Delhi.
The so-called god Pasupati is seated in the *paryankabandha asana*. According to the identification of
S.K. Ray, the surrounding six animals correspond with the six-faceted superimposed drawing of
the head of the seated god. He cannot be Siva who is a five-faceted *(pancha-mukha)* god. The figure
must then be the god of Kartikeya. Traditionally, Kartikeya, the six-faceted god *(saranana)*, is the
son of Lord Siva, but is also his teacher in the science of yoga.

94

Plate 61
Yogini. Bronze. Mohenjo-daro.
3000–2000 B.C. National Museum,
New Delhi.
An earliest example, wrongly identified
as dancing girl, of the yogini type which
persists over the years in varied forms—
virgins, yakshinis, surasundaris, apsaras,
nayikas, etc. She is in the *ahuyabarada
mudra*—yogini calling and offering
herself. The sequence of such archaic
ritual hand postures may have con-
tributed to the development of the later
elaborated dance mudras.

Plate 62
Yogini. Painted Wood. Orissa. c. 18th
century A.D. Asutosh Museum, Calcutta
University.
The tradition of yogini worship persists
through the ages and a number of
wooden figures, recently found, show
different types of mudras and bodily
positions. In this particular instance,
ahuyabarada mudra, the yogini calling
and offering herself—introspective in
her own enchantment—the dualism of
body and mind, flesh and spirit resolves
itself in a great serenity and poise:
"I am the Universal Female, inviting you
to unite with me." This is aided by the
dhyana formula, contemplative ritual
practice for invoking the image, con-
centrating on abstract attributes and
experiences.

तमः

"One must rise by that by which one falls"

Hevajra Tantra

Plates 63 and 64
Asanas. Painting. Palm-leaf Ms. Orissa. c. 17th century A.D.
Asana, a variation of the *angika* or bodily postures, mainly used in
meditation and sexo-yogic practices. The practice of asanas has
developed into a formidable series of esoteric positions that demand
great elasticity of body gained through long practice. In the act of
the physical process arrests "movement". Remaining still in asana,
while uniting with the object of love it evokes a state of perfect bliss.
Through the practice of asana supreme union is attained, the one
which combines both positive and negative aspects. There is no
coming in or going out, neither sin nor virtue can touch it. Such
realization of the ultimate within the self amounts to *moksha*,
liberation.

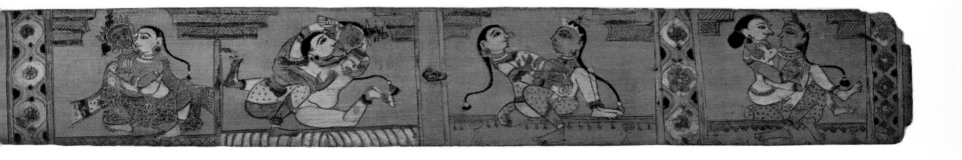

Plate 65
Yoni-asana. Stone. Khajuraho.
1059–1087 A.D. Photograph:
C.L.Vohra.
In this state, every conjunction of
opposites represents a transcending of
the phenomenal world, an abolition of
all experiences of duality.

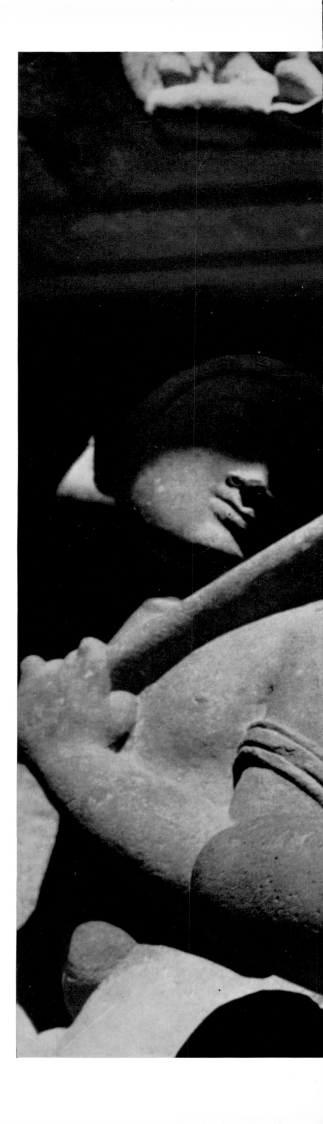

Plate 66
Mudra, detail of yoni-asana. Stone. Surya Temple, Konarak, Orissa. 1238–1264 A.D.
Photograph: Archaeological Survey of India.
The mudra, symbolic position of the hands, evokes an idea in the mind to emphasize
certain powers. By taking her in a particular stance, the completed asana terminates all
movement of the body reducing it to a single archetypal posture.

Plate 67
Yoni-asana. Painting. Nepal. c. 18th century. A.D. True mithuna happens to be the consummation of a long and difficult apprenticeship. After perfect control of the senses, one must approach the "devout woman" by stages and transubstantiate her into a goddess. No one can engage in the rite if he is not absolutely pure both spiritually as well as physically. In this state, every conjunction of opposites represents a transcendance of the phenomenal world, an abolition of all experience of duality. Such reintegration is the creative act, achieved by the *urdhareta* who makes the seed to rise to Sahasrara the abode of the primordial Male-Female (Siva-Sakti).

Plate 68
Sukhapadmasana.
Painting. Nepal.
c. 17th century. A.D.
In this bodily "knot"
formed by man and
woman in physical
unition, certain vital
centres in the body are
brought under com-
plete control. It per-
mits the performance
of secret "interior" acts
while on the exterior
the twin bodies remain
completely motionless.

Plate 69
Chanchalasana.
Painting. Nepal.
c. 17th century A.D.
The asana is one of
ease, in which the
adepts find identifica-
tion with self.

Plate 70
Adhomukhasana. Stone. Ranganayakula
Temple, Gandikota, Andhra Pradesh. c. 15th
century A.D. Photograph: Archaeological
Survey of India.
This asana is believed to increase youth, beauty
and energy. The ritual vessel on the yogini's
hand symbolizes onepointedness of mind.

Plate 71
Chakrasana. Painting. Nepal.
c. 18th century A.D.
To have its fullest effect the asana must be
accompanied by *mudras* (hand positions),
bandhas (contractions), *pranayam* (breath
control), *tratakac* visual concentration) and the
utterance of mantras. The practice of asana
in its advanced stages can be extremely
dangerous and is not be undertaken without
proper guidance.

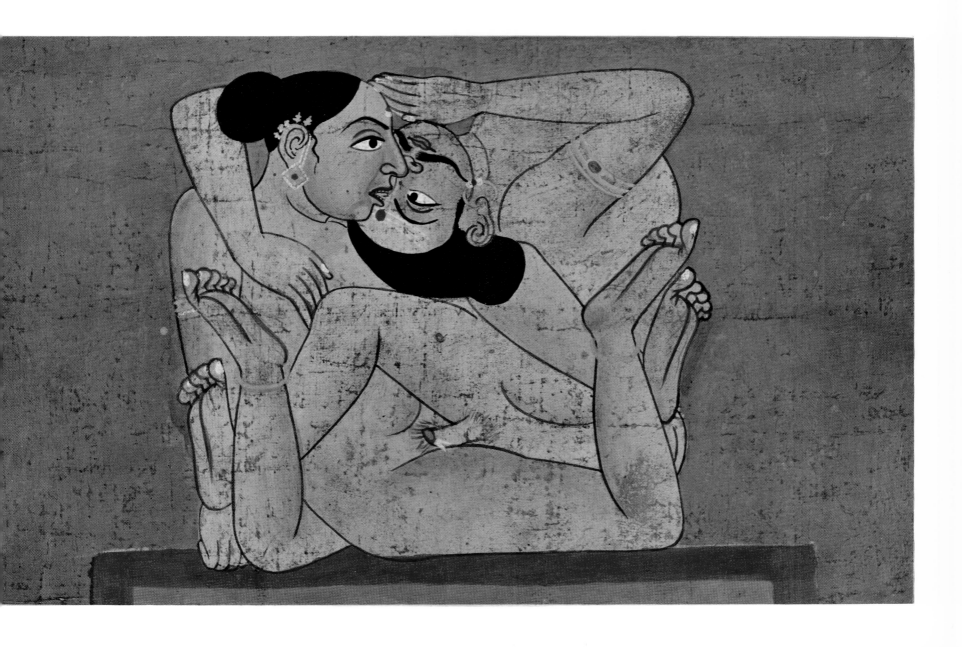

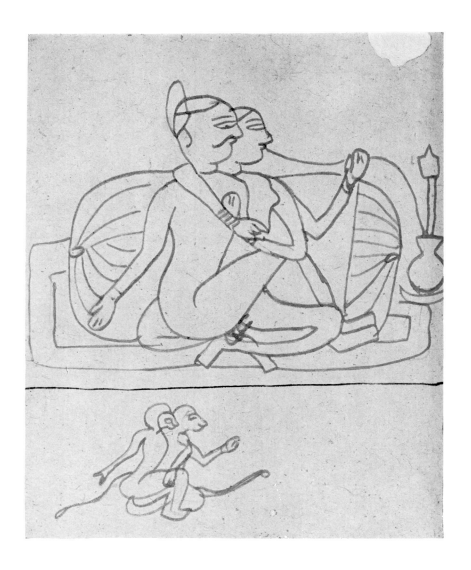

Plate 72
Bandara asana. Painting. Rajasthan.
c. 19th century A.D.
This type of asana—*bandara* (monkey)—
imitating the animal world, has been
used with a view to teaching a particular
position to the beginners. The gurus
adopted postures from the instructive
unchanging actions of the animals.

Plate 73
Monkey mithuna. Terracotta. Paharpur.
Rajshahi, North Bengal. c. 8–9th
century A.D. Photograph:
Archaeological Survey of India.

Plate 74
Ekadhari asana. Stone. Koilkuntola, Andhra Pradesh.
c. 12th century A.D. Photograph: Archaeological Survey of India.
Tremendous psychic energy is believed to be released by taking
a virgin into the Chakra-rite performed in tantric ceremonies.

Plate 75
Ekadhari asana. Painting. Rajasthan. c. 17th century A.D.
Various tantric ayurvedic formulas known to have rejuvenative
properties are sometimes used in the rituals. Alchemical potions
with purified mercury and gold are also often prepared.

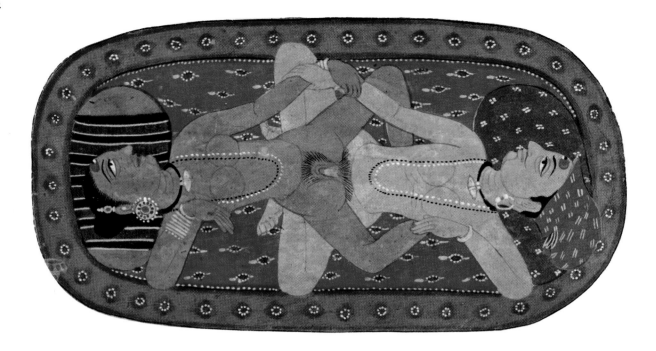

Plate 76
Janujugmasana. Painting. Nepal. c. 18th century A.D.
The adepts lie together with their heads at opposite ends, two open pair of legs fitted together like
two pincers in a way that the linga and the yoni come into the closest possible contact without
deep penetration. Since there are no violent muscular contractions, the pose helps in establishing
bodily intimacy in order to attain uniformity of psychic vibrations.

Plate 77
Puhapaka Asana. Painting. Rajasthan. c. 16th century A.D.
In this asana, a man and a woman unite with each other mouth to mouth. Their consciousness becomes
one with the unceasing consciousness of the universe thus eliminating the polarization of the bodies.
Lying on the back in a completely relaxed manner as if in a "corpse-like" position *(savasana)*
without any attempt at inducing orgasm by bodily motion, the interpenetration of the sexual energy
becomes a channel of the most vivid psychic experiences.

114

Plate 78
Siva-Sakti. Painting. Pahari style. Himachal Pradesh.
c. 18th century A.D. Photograph: Archaeological
Survey of India.
"What need have I of any outer woman? I have an
Inner Woman within myself." Kundalini is the
"Inner Woman", when struck, she shines like
"millions of lightning flashes" in the centre of the
sadhaka's body.

HRING, O destroyer of time!
SHRING, O terrific one!
KRING, Thou who art beneficent,
Possessor of all the arts,
Thou art Kamala,
Destroyer of the pride of the Kali Age,
Who art kind to him of the matted hair,
Devourer of Him who devours,
Mother of Time
Thou art brilliant as the fires of the final
dissolution,
Spouse of Him of the matted hair.
O Thou of formidable countenance,
Ocean of the nectar of compassion,
Merciful,
Vessel of mercy,
Whose mercy is without limit,
Who art attainable alone by Thy mercy,
Who art fire,
Tawny,
Black of hue,
Thou who increaseth the joy of the Lord
of creation,
Night of darkness,
In the form of desire,
Yet liberator from the bonds of desire.

Mahanirvana Tantra

Plate 79
Bhairavi. Stone. Markanda Temple, Chanda,
Maharashtra. c. 12th century A.D. Photograph:
Archaeological Survey of India.
Female bhairavis or yoginis may be widows, wives
of yogis, or kumaris (virgins), initiated at a very
early age. The left-handed tantric cult in particular
is closely associated with the Bhairavi sadhana.
In many instances, bhairavis are found to acquire
supernatural power through long meditation and
other yogic practices.

Plate 80
Bhairava. Painting. Deccani School. c. 18th
century A.D. Jagadish Mithal collection.
A Tantric Yogi, dark-skinned, red eyed, squatting on
a white asana, is listening to a raga, most probably
Bhairava, since Raga Bhairava's family colour for
distance is usually olive green and sky area bluish
grey, traversed by several currents of wavy greyish
white clouds. Siva's archetype is generally found in
the traditional representation of tantric Bhairava
which is shown as naked, with dishevelled or matted
hair, ash besmeared, wearing *rudraksha* garland and
pendant snake ear-rings *(kundala)* and sitting on a
tiger skin under a tree—absorbed in profound
meditation.

Plate 81
Dhumabati (detail). From an illuminated Ms. Nepal.
c. 1760 A.D. Bharat Kala Bhavan, Banaras.
Dhumabati, one of the most important goddesses
of the tantric ten Mahavidyas, is a manifestation of
Sakti in the process of creation, balance and dissolution. Dhumabati is pale in complexion
symbolizing upper spheres. She mounts a crow,
forever demanding material forms, at the same
time she renounces them by the process of absorbing
them in herself.

Plate 82
Devi. Painting. Kangra. Himachal Pradesh. c. 18th
century A.D.
Devi is known as Durga, Ambika, Bhavani, Kumari,
Vaishnavi, Parvati, personifying the Primordial One.
In the Devi Purana, Siva says to Parvati: "O
Daughter of Himalaya, I am white as the moon
and thou art dark. I am the sandal-tree, and thou art,
as it were, a snake entwined round it."

Siva-Sakti Yoga. Painting. Rajasthan. c. 18th century A.D. The human body parallels everything found in the macrocosm. The idea is to search for the whole truth within one's own self. Here, all the six chakras, the psychic centres, contained in the human body are conceived on the forehead. The ultimate object of an advanced yogi, after raising the Kundalini and piercing through the five elements, *panchabhutas*, namely, ether, air, fire, water and earth symbolised as Meru or Trikuta, the cosmic mountain, is encircled by the sakti power-field to denote the union of Sakti with Siva.

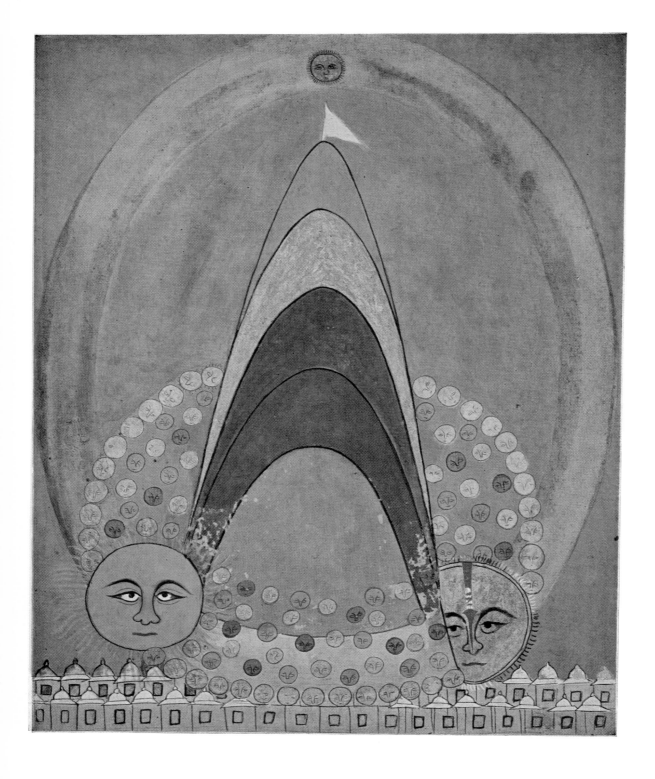

Plate 84
Sahasrara Chakra (detail). Painting. Rajasthan. c. 18th
century A.D.
Chakras are the chief circles through which the psychic
energy or *prana*, the vital life-force reaches the Sahasrara.
According to the Tantric doctrine, this centre lying outside
the body just above the crown of the head is of special
importance. It draws upon the cosmic force and thereby
supplies vital energy to the body.

Plate 85
Anahata Chakra (detail). Painting. Rajasthan. c. 18th
century A.D.
Anahata, the unstruck, is situated in the region of the
heart, *hridaya*. It has flaming red petals; its letters are
ka, kha, ga, gha, ha, cha, chha, ja, jha, na, ta, tha. When
Kundalini rises and reaches Anahata Chakra in her
journey upward, the devotee can hear the unstruck sound
or Anahata-dhvani which is the original *pranava* or cosmic
sound. It is generally taken to be the timeless sound-
symbol of the Supreme One.

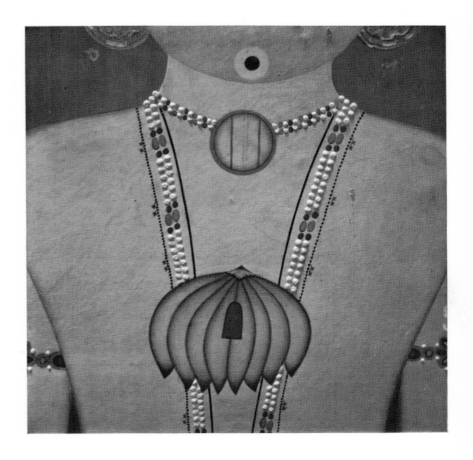

Plate 86

Chakras (detail). From an illuminated Ms. Nepal.
c. 17th century A.D. Bharat Kala Bhavan, Banaras.
Chakra or the circle of energy is the psychic body at
its point of contact with the physical body. There are
about thirty chakras mentioned in the texts. Of these,
six, lying within, and one outside the body, are of
special significance and make up the seven major
chakras.

Each major chakra is associated with sound and colour
as represented by the Sanskrit alphabet. Each has a
certain number of petals, its own characteristic colour,
distinctive geometrical design, a male deity, a sakti
and the mystic seed syllable, to be meditated upon.
The major chakras are shown here from bottom as
Muladhara, Svadhishthana, Manipura, Anahata, Visuddha, Ajna and finally Kundalini reaching Sahasrara.
Kundalini is the name of the reserve of psychic energy
symbolized by the serpent which lies in a state of
trance coiled around the Svayambhu-linga, the so-called
subtle centre, which occupy a point near the base of
the spine at the Muladhara plexus.

In most cases the Kundalini lies dormant throughout
one's life-time. Only prolonged yogic training and
disciplines can rouse the Kundalini to consciousness.
Once roused the Kundalini can be directed by a subtle
nerve to start her journey up the Sushumna, the central
channel corresponding to the principles of the sun,
moon and fire, and pierce through the various chakras,
acquiring unlimited power for the initiate (Sadhaka).

Plate 87
Muladhara Chakra (detail). Painting. Rajasthan. c. 18th century A.D.
Muladhara lies almost at the bottom of the spine; it is the lowest centre of the human body, a little above
the anus and behind the penis. Muladhara, being the root-foundation, is the centre in which most of the
subtle arteries are rooted, and from which point they spread throughout the body. Its element is earth.
The Svyambhu linga is the fiery triangle in the centre which is encircled by the coiled Kundalini.

Plate 88
Mahadevi. Painting. Kangra, Himachal Pradesh. c. 18th century A.D.
Mahadevi is also known as Kalika because she is without any
beginning or end; her body is the all pervading blue colour of the
universe. Though herself changeless, she binds all beings *(jivas)* by
bonds of *maya*, symbolized by her dishevelled hair. Her earrings are
formed of the two tiny *sadhakas*, signifying that the child-like *sadhakas*
are dear to her. She is the sole creator, preserver and destroyer of
infinite millions of worlds; her nakedness symbolises creation, her
full and high breasts denote preservation, and a terrible expression on
her face significes the withdrawal from all things. As she devours all
existence, her white teeth indicate pure self-manifesting, Sattva-guna
supressing the mass of blood which is Rajas and Tamas. Her form is
that of Sattva, Rajas, Tamas (Being—Consciousness—Bliss), and her
true nature stands for eternal liberation; she wears a girdle of human
heads to indicate disentangled elements in their pure state.

Plate 89
Nairita. Stone. Chanduwar, Orissa. c. 9–10th century A.D. Indian Museum, Calcutta.
Nairita, Lord of the North-East quarter, is one of the Ashtadikapalas or guardians of the eight
quarters. He is mounted on a human corpse, *nara-vahana*.

Plate 90
Mahakali or Nairatma (?) Painting. Kangra, Himachal Pradesh. c. 18th century A.D.
Though the goddess does not exactly conform to the description of Nairatma given in the
Sadhanmala, there are distinguishing features which identify her as the goddess Mahakali
resembling the Chandika-sakti, particularly Chamunda as well as Vaishnavi.
Mahakali sits on a corpse. If the corpse lies on its back the goddess is Nairatma. According
to her *dhyana:* "the face looks terrible with base fangs and a protruding tongue; she carries
the Kartri in the right hand and bears the Kapala and the Khatvanga in the left. Her eyes are
red and round, and she is endowed with the five auspicious symbols."

Plate 91

Chandi. Painting. Rajasthan. c. 18th century A.D.

Chandi is the same as Durga, the loving and protecting Mother, who in a different aspect in the form of Kali is responsible for annihilation. Then she dons a garland of *gyana-mala* of human heads to symbolize her wisdom and power. These heads are generally fifty in number representing the fifty letters of the Sanskrit alphabet, which are the outer manifestations of Sabda Brahma or Brahma in the form of Sound. Kali's lolling tongue showing blood red colour signifies the Raja-guna (energy) whose circular movement gives impetus to all creative activities. By this specific gesture, she is exhorting the *sadhakas* to control their Raja-guna. The sacrificial sword and the severed head held by the left hand are the symbols of dissolution. Darkness and death are by no means the mere absence of light and life, rather their origin. The *sadhaka* worships the cosmic power in its female form—for she represents the kinetic aspect, the masculine being the static which is activated only through her power.

← Plate 92
Saptamundi-asana. Painting. Mandi, Himachal Pradesh. c.18th
century A.D.
In Tantric sadhana, the most difficult meditative and occult practices
are performed when one sits in Padmasana on human skulls. Five
skulls known as Panchamundi are required for this esoteric position.
Here Devi is practising an asana, seated on the seven-skulls (Saptamundi). According to Tantra, brain is the most important reservoir
of forces controlling the unconscious. Since the skull is directly in
touch with this reservoir, many astonishing *siddhis* or supernatural
powers come to those who can meditate sitting on *panchamundi* or
saptamundi.

Plate 93
Bhairavi or Kali. Painting. Mandi, Himachal Pradesh.
c. 18th century A.D.
Bhairavi or Kali, personifying the divine energy of Siva, wears a
garland of severed heads *(mundamala)*; in two of her hands she holds
a sword and a seed-cup, representing her destructive and creative
aspects, while the other two dispel fear and exhort to spiritual strength.

Plate 94
Garuda. Painting. Kangra, Himachal Pradesh. c. 18th century A.D.
Garuda, a mythical bird, is the mount of Vishnu. Half giant and half
eagle, with the body and limbs of a man, he has the head, beak and
talons of an eagle. Such was his radiance that the gods mistook him
for Agni, the god of fire. The association of Garuda with snakes is
emphasised in the epics and the Puranas, and is also illustrated in his
earlier and medieval representations. Though connected with Vishnu,
in this representation the depiction of Saivite and Sakta forms as well
combined to make him the manifestation of supreme power.

Plate 95
Gunatraya Chakrasana. From an illuminated Ms. Nepal. c. 17th
century A.D.
Asana is visualized as the pattern of forces *sattva*, *rajas*, and *tamas*,
symbolized by the colours yellow, red and black along with the
colourless white of cosmic consciousness—that principle which
stays forever motionless, yet acts through its own radiation—,
generates all forms of manifestation. The squares complete the
suggestion that all this is 'within'.

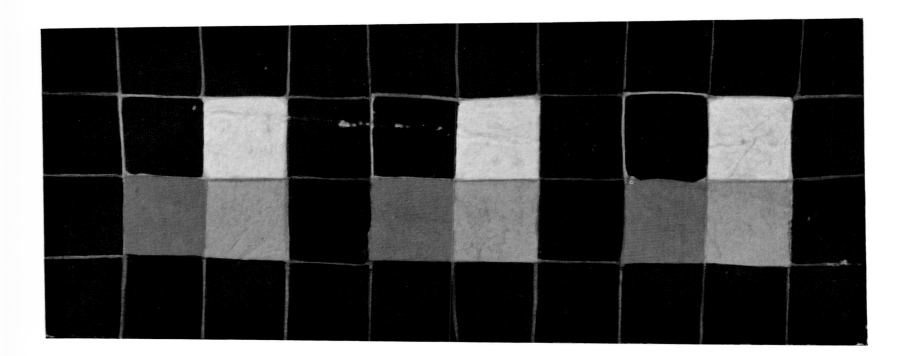

Plate 96 →

← Plate 96
Jambu-dvipa (detail). Painting. Gujrat. c. 17th century A.D.
Indicating aggregation of stars.

Plate 97
Pure Consciousness. From an illuminated Ms. Gujarat. c. 1700 A.D.
Museum and Picture Gallery, Baroda.
Sat, Chit, Ananda—Pure Being, Consciousness and Bliss. In its pure
existence the cosmic process has reverted to entropy. The vibration
begins anew and the creative impulse in the cosmic process starts.
"Tantric discipline is in its nature a synthesis. It has seized on the large
universal truth that there are two poles of being whose essential unity
is the secret of existence..." In this way, the Tantric rituals are the
basis of many a philosophy—Hindu, Jaina or Buddhist. In fact, the
Tantric method of Sadhana (spiritual discipline) has been in vogue since
pre-Harrappan culture, c. 3000 B.C. The Tantric doctrines also
crossed into China, Tibet and elsewhere from India around 400 A.D.

Select Bibliography

ABHYANKAR, KASHINATH VASUDEV
Sakta-Darsana of Hayagriva. Poona, Sanskrit Vidya Parishamstha, 1966.

AGRAWALA, V. S.
Matsya Purana—a study. Varanasi All India Kashiraj Trust, 1963.

ANAND, MULK RAJ and HUTHEESING, KRISHNA
The Brides Book of Beauty. Bombay, Kutub, 1947.

ASHTAVAKRA SAMHITA
Text with English Translation. Mayavati, Published by Advaita Ashrama, 1958.

ASIATIC RESEARCHES
or Transaction of the Society, instituted in Bengal. Calcutta, B. L. Doss, n. d. Vol. II.

AUROBINDO, SRI
Foundations of Indian Culture, Pondichéry, Sri Aurobindo Ashram, 1968.
(The) Future Evolution of Man. London, Allen & Unwin, 1963.
(The) Human Cycle. The ideal of Human Unity, War and Self-determination. Pondichéry, Sri Aurobindo Ashram, 1962.
On Yoga. The synthesis of Yoga. Pondichéry, Sri Aurobindo Ashram, 1965.

AVADHUT
Nilakantha Himalaya. Calcutta, Mitra & Ghosh, 1372 B. S. (Bengali).

AVADHUTA, ACHARYA VIMUKTANANDA
Cosmic Society—An Anthology. New Delhi, Renaissance Publ.

AYYANGAR, T. R. SRINIVASA
Yoga Upanishads. Madras, Adyar Library, 1952.

BANERJEE, J. N.
Pauranic and Tantric Religion. Calcutta University, 1966.

BANERJEE, AKSHYA KUMAR
Sadhya-Sadhan Tattva-Vichar. Calcutta, A.K. Datta Gupta, 1327 B. S. in 2 parts (Bengali).

BECKETT, L. C.
Unbounded Worlds. London, the Ark Press, n. d.

BESANT, ANNIE and LEADBEATER, C.W.
Occult Chemistry. Adyar, Theosophical Publ. House, 1951.

BHAGAVAD-GITA
A new Translation and Commentary with Sanskrit Text, by His Highness Maharishi Mahesh Yogi. London, International S.Q.M. publ., 1967.

BHAGAVAD-GITA
trad. française par Sylvain Levi et J.-T. Stickney, Paris Adrien Maisonneuve, 1938.

BHARATI, AGEHANANDA
Tantric Tradition. London, Rider & Co., 1965.

BHATTACHARYA, BIDHUSEKHAR
Gauda Padiyam Agam Shastram. Calcutta University, 1950.

BHATTACHARYA, SURENDRANATH
Hatayoga Sadhan. Calcutta, Sulabh Library, 1358 B. S. (Bengali).

BHATTACHARYA, SURENDRA NATH
Rakshasi Tantra. Calcutta, Town Library, 1356 B. S. (Bengali).

BONESTELL, CHESLEY and LEY, WILLY
The Conquest of Space. London, Sidgwick & Jackson, 1950.

BRONOWSKI, J.
Science and Human Value. London, Penguin, 1964.

CAYCEDO, ALFONSO
Indian of Yogis. Delhi, National Publishing House, 1966.

CHAKRAVARTI, SURESHCHANDRA
Human Life and Beyond. Calcutta University, 1947.

CHATTOPADHAYA, PRAMOD KUMAR
Avadhuta O Yogisanga. Calcutta, Bhattacharya & Sons, 1951 (Bengali).

CHATTOPADHAYA, RASIK MOHAN
Bhuta Damar. Calcutta, S. N. Mukherjee, 1338 B. S. (Bengali) Satkarma Dipika. Calcutta, Sanskrit Pustak Bhandar, 1338 B. S. (Bengali).

CHOUDHARY, RADHAKRISHNA
Vratyas in Ancient India. Varanasi, Chowkhamba Sanskrit Series, 1964.

CHUNG-YUAN, CHANG
Creativity and Taoism. New York, The Julian Press, n. d.

COLLIER, GRAHAM
Form, Space and Vision. Englewood Cliffs, Prentice Hall, 1964.

COOMARASWAMY, ANANDA K.
Buddha and the Gospel of Buddhism. New York, Harper, 1964.

DANIELOU, ALAIN
Hindu Polytheism. London, Routledge, 1964.
L'Érotisme Divinisé. Paris, Editions Buchet-Chastel, 1962.

DAS GUPTA, TAMONASH CHANDRA
Aspects of Bengali Society from old Bengali Literature. Calcutta University, 1935.

DATTA, BIBHUTIBHUSHAN
History of Hindu Mathematics. Bombay, Asia Publishing House, 1962.

DE BARY, WILLIAM THEODORE
Sources of Indian Tradition. New York, Columbia University Press, 1958.

DE, SUSHIL KUMAR
Treatment of Love in Sanskrit Literature. Calcutta, S.K.Das, 1929.

DURANT, WILL
Story of Civilization. N.Y. Simon Schuster, 1942. Part I Our Oriental Heritage.

EDGERTON, FRANKLIN
The Beginnings of Indian Philosophy. London, Allen & Unwin, 1965.

EVANS-WENTZ, W.Y.
Le livre des morts du Tibet, Paris, Adrien-Maisonneuve, 1958.
Yoga tibétain et doctrines secrètes, Paris, Adrien-Maisonneuve, 1938.

FRANKS, HERBERT W.
Sinnbild der Chemie (Microstructure of Chemistry). Basel, Switzerland, Basilius Press A.G., 1968.

FREDERIC, LOUIS
La Danse Sacrée De L'Inde. Paris, Arts et Métiers Graphics, 1956.

GAMOW, GEORGE
One two three—Infinity. N.Y., Bantam, 1967.

GIBSON, WALTER B. and GIBSON, LITZKA R.
The complete Illustrated Book of The Psychic Science, London, Corgi Books, 1969.

GRAUBARD, MARK
Foundations of Life Science. New York, D. Van Nostrand, 1965.

HARGREAVES, F.J.
The Size of the Universe. London, Penguin Books, 1947.

HINDU ART OF LOVE
Richard Burton's Translation of the Ananga Ranga and The Symposium of Plato. Tr. by B. JOWETT. London, Kimber Pocket Ed., 1963.

INDIAN INSTITUTE OF ADVANCED STUDY
Indian Aesthetics and Art Activity. Simla, Indian Institute of Advanced Studies, 1968.

INGALLS, DANIEL H.H.
An Anthology of Sanskrit Court Poetry. Vidyakara's Subhasitaratnakosa. Cambridge, Harvard Univ. Press, 1969.

INGELMAN, SUNDBERG, AXEL and LENNART, NILSSON
Child is born. New York, Seymour Laurence, 1966.

IRVING, ROBERT
Sound and Ultrasonics London, Dennis Dobson, 1959.

JAGADGURU SWAMI SRI BHARATI KRISNA
Vedic Mathematics. Banaras Hindu University, 1965.

JENNY, HANS
Cymatics. Basel, Basilius Press, 1967.

JISL, LUMIR
Tibetan Art. London, Spring Books, n.d.

JUNG, C.G.
Memories, Dreams, Reflections. N.Y., Pantheon Books, 1963

KALYANA MALLA
Ananga Ranga Tr. & annotated by F.F. Arbuthnot & Richard Burton. Medical Press, N.Y. 1964.

KANDINSKY
Kandinsky The Colour. Library of Art. By Frank Whitford. London,
Paul Hamlyn, 1967.

KANE, PANDURANG VAMAN
History of Dharmasastra. Vol.V. Pt.II. Puranas and Dharmasastra:
Tantras and Dharmasastra,
Poona, Bhandarkar Oriental Research Institute, 1962.

KANWAR LAL
The Cult of Desire. Delhi, Asia Press, 1966.

KAULACARA, RAMCHANDRA
Silpa Prakasa. Tr. Ed. by Alice Bonar and Sadasiva Rath Sarma.
Leiden, Brill, 1966.

KAVIRAJ, GOPINATH
Aspects of Indian thought. University of Burdwan, 1966.
Sadhudarshan O Sat Prasanga. Calcutta, S.Mukherjee, 1369 B.S.
in 2 parts. Calcutta, Prachi Publs., 1370 B.S. (Bengali).
Tantra O Agam Shastrer Digdarshan. Calcutta, Sanskrit College, 1963
(Bengali).
Tantrick Bangmoy me Sakta Drishti. Patna, Bihar Rashtrabhasa.
Parishad, 1963 (in Hindi).

KEPES, GYORGY
The Nature and Art of Motion. London, Studio Vista, 1965.

KOKKOKA
(Hindu Secrets of Love) Rati Rahasya. Tr. by S.C.Upadhyaya.
Bombay, Taraporevala, 1965.
The Koka Shastra being the Ratirahasya of Kokkoka and other
medieval Indian writings on love. Tr. with an introduction by Alex
Comfort. London, Allen & Unwin, 1964.

KOKKOKAM & RATI RAHASYAM
Kokkokam & Rati Rahasyam. Ed. by T.N.Ray. Calcutta, Medical
Book Company, 1960.

KONOW, STEN and TUXEN POUL
The Religions of India. Copenhagen, G.E.C.Gad Publ. 1942.

KRAMRISCH, STELLA
(The) Art of Nepal. N.Y., The Asia Society, 1968.

KUVALAYANANDA, SWAMI
Asanas, Bombay, Popular Prakashan, 1964.

LEESON, FRANCIS
Kama Shilpa. Bombay, Taraporevala, 1962.

LIN YUTANG
Wisdom of India. London, Michael Joseph, 1948.

MAHESH YOGI, MAHARISHI
The Science of Being and Art of Living. London, International S.R.M.
Publications, 1966.

MARCADE, JEAN
Eros Kalos. Erotic Elements in Greek Art. Geneva, Nagel Publishers,
1962.
Roma Amor. Geneva, Nagel Publishers, 1961.

MARKS, ROBERT W. (Ed.)
Great Ideas of Modern Science. N.Y., Bantam Science, 1967.

MASTERS, ROBERT E.L. and HOUSTON, JEAN
Psychedelic Art. London, Weidenfeld, 1968.

MUKERJEE, RADHAKAMAL
History of Indian Civilization. Bombay, Hind Kitabs, 1966. 2 Vols.

NAWAB, SARABHAI MUNILAL
Mahaprabharika Navasmaran. Ahmedabad, Shree Jain Prachina
Sahityadhar Granthabali.
Series No.6, 1961 (in Gujarati).

NAWAB, VIDYA SARABHAI
419 illustrations of Indian Music & Dance in Western Indian Style.
Ahmedabad, Sarabhai Manilal Nawab, 1964.

O'RELLY, EDWARD
Sexercises. New York, Pocket Book, 1966.

PANDIT, M.P.
Kundalini Yoga. Madras, Ganesh Co., 1962.
Studies in the Tantras and the Veda. Madras, Ganesh & Co., 1967.

PANDEY, KANTI CHANDRA
Abhinavagupta—An Historical and Philosophical Study. Varanasi,
Chowkhamba Sanskrit Series, 1963.

PATANJALI
Yoga-Sutra. Tr. from Sanskrit by Bengali Baba. Poona,
N.R.Bhargawa, 1949.

Yoga-System of Patanjali. Tr. from the original Sanskrit by James Hughton Woods. Delhi, Motilal Banarasidas, 1966.

POPPER, FRANK
Origins and Development of Kinetic Art. Tr. from French by Stephen Bann. London, Studio Vista, 1968.

POTT, P.H.
Yoga and Yantra. The Hague, Martinus Nijhoff, 1966.

PRATYAGATMANANDA SARASWATI
Fundamentals of Vedanta Philosophy. Madras, Ganesh & Co., 1961.

RADHAKRISHNAN, S.
The Brahma Sutra. The Philosophy of Spiritual Life. London, Allen & Unwin, 1960

RAVAL, P.D.
Atomic Theory in the Vedas. Published by the Author at Morvi, 1964.

RAY, SANKARNATH
Bharater Sadhak. Calcutta, Writers Syndicate, 1337 B.S. Part V–VII (Bengali).

RANDHAWA, M.S.
Kangra Valley Painting. India Govt. Pub. Division, 1954.

RAWSON, PHILIP
Erotic Art of the East. Introduction by Alex Comfort. New York, Putnam, 1968.

REYNA, RUTH
The Philosophy of Matter in the Atomic Era. Bombay, Asia Publishing House, 1962.

REICH, WILHELM
The Function of the Orgasm. London, Panther, 1968.

ROSS, NANCY WILSON
Three Ways of Asian Wisdom. New York. Simon & Schuster, 1966.

RUSSELL, BERTRAND
Marriage and Morals. New York, Bantam Books, 1966.

SAKTA PRAMOD
Compiled by Raja Devanandana Sinha Bahadur. Ed. by Pandit Rashwraj Dubeji. Bombay, Sri Venkateshwar State Press, 1904.

SATPREM
Sri Aurobindo or Adventure of Consciousness. Pondicherry, Sri Aurobindo Ashram, 1968.

SATYANANDA SARASWATI
Kamaka Kumari Puja, Halisahar, Brahmachari Syamachaitanya, 1360 B.S. (Bengali).

SATYA PRAKASH
Founders of Sciences in Ancient India. New Delhi, Ancient Scientific Studies, 1965.

SCHRADER, F. OTTO
Introduction to Pancaratna and The Ahirbudhya Samhita. Madras, Adyar Library, 1916.

SCHWENK, THEODOR
Sensitive Chaos. The Creation of Flowing Forms in Water and Air. London, Rudolf Steinu Press, 1965.

SEN, K.M.
Hinduism. London, Penguin, 1961.

SEN, R.K.
Aesthetic Enjoyment. Calcutta University, 1966.

SHIVANANDA SARASWATI
Yogic Therapy, Kamakhya, Umachal Prakashani, 1957.

SIDDHESWARANANDA SWAMI
Meditation according to Yoga Vedanta. Trichur, Sri Ramakrishna Ashram, 1966.

SIERKSMA, F.
Tibet's Terrifying Deities. Sex and Aggression in religious Occulturation. Rutland, Charles E. Tuttle & Co., 1966.

SINGH, JAGJIT
Great Ideas and Theories of Modern Cosmology, 1961.

SINGH, MADANJEET
Himalayan Art. UNESCO Art Books, London, Macmillan, 1965.

SIVARAMAMURTI, C.
Sanskrit Literature and Art—Memoirs of Indian Culture (Memoir of the Arch. Survey of India, No. 73). Calcutta, Government of India Press, 1955.

SPENCER, SIDNEY
Mysticism. London, Penguin Books, 1967.

STREET, ROBERT
Modern Sex Techniques. New York, Lancer Books, 1966.

SWAMIJI, MAHARAJ
Tantric Panchanka. Prayag, Kalyan Mandir (Hindi).

TABORI PAUL
Pictorial History of Love. London, Spring Books, 1966.

TAYLOR, G. RATTRAY
Sex in History, London, Panther Books, 1965.

THOMAS, P.
Incredible India. Bombay, Taraporevala & Co., 1966.
Kama Kalpa or The Hindu Ritual of Love. Bombay, Taraporevala, 1963.

THORNS, SABINA
Precepts for Perfection. Madras, Ganesh & Co., 1961.

VAIDYA, R. V.
Astronomical Light on Vedic Culture. Bombay, Makarand Sahitya, 1965.

VANDER, A. WILLY L. & Others
The Encyclopaedia of Sex Practice. London, Francis Aldon, n.d.

VATSYAYANA
Kama Sutra (Eng. Tr.). Delhi, Asia Press, 1967.
Kama Sutra. Ed. by H. S. Gamber. Bombay, Brijmohan & Co., n.d.
The Kama Sutra Tr. by Richard Burton and F. F. Arbuthnot. London, Allen & Unwin, 1965.
Kama Sutra. Illustrated Edition. Ed. & Tr. into English by S. C. Upadhyaya. Bombay, Taraporevala, 1963.
Le Kama Soutra de Vatsyayana. Trad. Française de I. Liseux. Paris, J. Fort, éd.

VIDYA PRAKASH
Khajuraho. Bombay, Taraporevala, 1967.

VIDYARATNA, KALI PRASANNA
Brihattantra Kosha. Calcutta, Ganesh Ch. Ghose, B.S. 1295.

VIDYARATNA, RAKHAL CHANDRA
Kalpavalli. I–IV Parts. Published by the author. Manbhum, Pancha-koth, 1343 B.S.

VISHNUDEVANANDA, SWAMI
The Complete Illustrated Book of Yoga. New York, Julian Press, 1961.

VIVEKANANDA, SWAMI
The Yogas and other works including Jnana-Yoga, Bhakti-Yoga, Karma-Yoga, Raja-Yoga, Talks, Lectures, Poems and Letters. New York, Ramakrishna-Vivekananda Centre, 1953.

VOLIN, MICHAEL and PHETAN NANCY
Sex and Yoga. London, Pelham Book, 1967.

WADIYAR, SRI JAYA CHAMARAJA BAHADUR
An Aspect of Indian Aesthetics. University of Madras, 1956.

WALKER, BENJAMIN
Hindu World. London, Allen & Unwin, 1968. 2 Vols.

WOOD, EARNEST
Yoga. London, Cassell, 1962.

WOODROFFE, SIR JOHN
Introduction to Tantra Sashtra. Madras, Ganesh & Co., 1969.
La puissance du serpent, Lyon, Ed. Paul Derain, 1959.
Principles of Tantra, Madras, Ganesh & Co., 1914.
The world as Power, Madras, Ganesh & Co., 1966.
The great liberation (Mahanirvana Tantra), Madras, Ganesh & Co., 1963.
Kularnava Tantra, Madras, Ganesh & Co., 1965.
The Garland of letters, Madras, Ganesh & Co., 1969.
Hymns to the goddess, Madras, Ganesh & Co., 1964.
Hymn to Kali (Karpuradi-stotra), Ganesh & Co., 1965.
Sakti and Sakta, Ganesh & Co., 1965.

YOGANANDA, PARAMAHANSA
Autobiography of a Yogi. London, Rider & Co., 1961.

YOGINI TANTRA
Ganga Vishnu Srikrishnadasa. Bombay. n.d.

YOUNG, J. Z. and MARGERISON, TOM. Ed.
The Explosion of Science—from Molecule to Man. London, Thames & Hudson, 1967.

YOUNG, WAYLAND
Eros Denied. London, Weidenfeld & Nicolson, 1965.

ZIMMER HEINRICH
Philosophies of India, New York, Pantheon Books, 1951.
Mythes et symboles dans l'art et la civilisation de l'Inde, Paris, Payot, 1951.

Journal

HIPPIE SEX FREEDOM MOVEMENT
By Leonard H. Gross (in Sexology, New York, Jan., 1968).

SEX AND THE ARTS
Explosive Scene (in Newsweek, New York, April 14, 1969).

Hymn to the Goddess

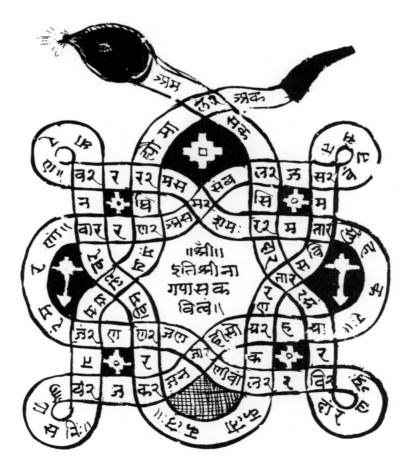

Muladhara chakra

1

Thus shall I pray to Thee, O Tripurā,
To attain the fruit of my desires,
In this hymn by which men attain that Lakshmī,
Who is worshipped by the Devas.

2

Origin of the world thou art,
Yet hast Thou Thyself no origin,
Though with hundreds of hymns.
Even Brahmā, Vishnu, and Maheshvara cannot know Thee
Therefore we worship Thy breasts, Mother of all Shāstra,
Shining with fresh saffron.

3

O Tripurā, we adore Thee,
Whose body shines with the splendour of a thousand risen suns,
Holding with two of thy hands a book and a rosary of rudrāksha
beads,
And with two others making the gestures
Which grant boons and dispel fear.
With three lotus eyes is Thy lotus face adorned,
Beauteous is Thy Neck with its necklace of large pearls.

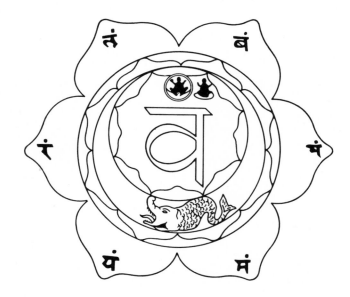

Svadhishthana chakra

4

O Mother, how can the ignorant, whose minds are restless with
    doubt and dispute,
Know Thy form ravishing with its vermilion,
Stooping with the weight of Thy breasts,
Accessible only by merit,
Acquired in previous births?

5

O Bhavānī, the munis describe thee in physical form;
The Shruti speaks of Thee in subtle form;
Others call Thee presiding Deity of speech;
Others, again, as the root of the worlds.
But we think of Thee
As the untraversable ocean of mercy, and nothing else.

6

Worshippers contemplate Thee in their heart
As three-eyed, adorned with the crescent moon,
White as the autumnal moon,
Whose substance is the fifty letters,
Holding in Thy hands a book, a rosary, a jar of nectar, and
    making the vyakhya mudrā.

Manipura chakra

7

O Tripurā, Thou art Shambhu united with Parvati.
Thou art now Vishnu embraced by Kamalā,
And now Brahmā born of the lotus.
Thou art again the presiding Devī of speech,
And yet again art the energy of all these.

8

I, having taken refuge with the four—
Bhāvas, Parā, and others born of the vāgbhava (bīja),
Shall never in my heart forget Thee, the supreme Devatā,
Whose substance is existence and intelligence,
And who expresseth by Thy throat and other organs
The Bhāva appearing in the form of letters.

9

The blessed, having conquered the six enemies,
And drawing in their breath,
With steady mind fix their gaze on the tip of their nostrils,
And contemplate in their head Thy moon-crested form,
Resplendent as the newly risen sun.

Anahata chakra

10

The Vedas proclaim that Thou createth the world,
Having assumed the other half of the body of the enemy of Kāma,
Verily is it true, O Daughter of the mountain and the only
    World-mother,
That had this not been so,
The multitude of worlds would never have been.

11

In company with the wives of the Kinnaras,
The Siddha women, whose eyes are reddened by wine
Having worshipped Thee with the flowers of celestial trees
In Thy pītha in the caverns of the golden mountain,
Sing Thy praises.

12

I worship in my heart the Devī whose body is moist with nectar,
Beauteous as the splendour of lightning,
Who, going from Her abode to that of Shiva,
Opens the lotuses on the beautiful way of the sushumna.

Vishuddha chakra

13

O Tripurā, I take refuge at Thy lotus feet,
Worshipped by Brahmā, Vishnu, and Maheshvara;
The abode of bliss, the source of the Vedas,
The origin of all prosperity.
Thou whose body is Intelligence itself.

14

I shall never forget Her who is the giver of happiness;
She it is, O Mother, who, in the form of the Moon,
Creates the world full of sounds and their meanings,
And again, by Her power in the form of the Sun,
She it is who maintains the world.
And She, again, it is who, in the form of Fire, destroys the
    whole universe at the end of the ages.

15

Men worship Thee under various names—
As Nārāyana; as She who saves from the ocean of Hell;
As Gauri; as the allayer of grief; as Sarasvati,
And as the three-eyed giver of knowledge.

Ajna chakra

16

O Mother of the world, such as worship Thee with twelve Verses
of this hymn attain to Thee, and gain all powers of speech
and the supreme abode.

Bhairavistotra
TANTRASARA

Sahasrara chakra

Printed in Switzerland
Basler Druck- und Verlagsanstalt, Basel

Colour Plates: The Radiant Process, Calcutta
Binding: Max Grollimund, Reinach, Switzerland